YOU AND YOUR SHIPS

Genial Jim Davis
Mine Host at the must-go IMIF dinner
From Seatrade Review, *December 1997*

You and Your Ships

by

Jim Davis CBE K(DK)

The Memoir Club

© James Davis 2006

First published in 2006 by
The Memoir Club
Stanhope Old Hall
Stanhope
Weardale
County Durham

British Library Cataloguing in
Publication Data.
A catalogue record for this book
is available from the
British Library

ISBN: 1-84104-151-3

Typeset by TW Typesetting, Plymouth, Devon
Printed by CPI Antony Rowe, Eastbourne

*To my wonderful wife Hanny
and our three girls Mariske,
Katrina and Charlotte*

Contents

List of Illustrations

Preface: 'You and Your Ships'

I was inspired to attempt this short autobiography by a friend of mine, Peter Bowring CBE, whose own delightfully written story I had read. He said I should write mine. When I protested that I did not think my own life could possibly interest anyone he totally disagreed saying: 'You are wrong. I am sure your varied career would be of great interest and even if it were not you would leave something much cherished by your *family*.'

The title I have chosen is not original. It was used for a short war-time paperback written by A.C. Hardy – an enthusiast for motor propulsion of large vessels against the prevailing taste for steam turbines. The book was by no means a best-seller and has, apart from by me and possibly Laurence Dunn who illustrated it, been long forgotten.

I wanted the title because it was said to me by my dear mother who, slightly exasperated, saw and heard me constantly drawing, writing and talking about 'ships'. In those years – from three or four years old onwards I guess – I never was happy when far away from the sea and ships. And a lifetime in the profession has still not cured me.

This potted life story is a product only of my memory. I was not and am not one to keep a diary. It has been quite a task and a slightly disconcerting feature is that it revives in my mind some of the less happy days and less happy situations in both business and, occasionally, private life.

A nice feature of the human psyche is that we tend to forget the bad times and push them to the background and remember only the good. However when writing a sequential 'life' of this type one inevitably recalls slights and the like which would be better forgotten! I really hope that some of my more trenchant comments on certain individuals do not appear to be in any way spiteful. The record would not however be complete without some of them and I must just hope that they do not spoil description of a genuinely fortunate and happy life.

I have been much blessed. Though not making me rich, the great Shipping Industry has enabled me to make friends (not just acquaintances) all over the world. There have been setbacks – in all conscience who does not have them? – but all has so far worked out well and my prime achievement has been a wonderful family.

Jim Davis

CHAPTER 1

Early days

I T ALL STARTED for me on 20 July 1928, the day I was born in 'Summer Lawn', Dovercourt.

Dovercourt being the 'residential' area adjoining the ancient Port of Harwich, my father was the 'Boss' – various descriptions from Marine Superintendent to Shipping Director evolved to describe his position in the LNER (later British Rail) cross North Sea services from Harwich to Holland (the Hook), Antwerp, Zeebrugge (train and passenger ferries) and Rotterdam. Father was a highly respected man. Being a youngest son, very early orphaned by the premature death of his parents, he had – I feel to escape a confining boyhood under a head mistress maiden aunt – gone to sea as an apprentice in sail. He gained his Master's ticket in sail and steam. Nine times round Cape Horn and six times round the world under sail was a record of his early years at sea, which included being shipwrecked by a nitrates over-heating fire which destroyed *Marion Fraser*, a full rigged ship of which he was – I believe – third mate at the time. No benign employers existed in those days and he had to make his own way back from Chile as a DBS (Distressed British Seaman).

Via the Army ('Movements' in the Royal Engineers) and where he was awarded an MBE (Military) for services in the Irish 'Troubles' he had made his way to becoming General Manager of the Train Ferry Service (Société Belgo-Anglaise des Ferry Boats) which ran between Richborough Kent and Zeebrugge. From there he was selected to be LNER's Marine Chief.

During the 1939–45 War he was, successively, a Colonel (Movements) in the Royal Engineers and later Assistant Director of Sea Transport at the Ministry of War Transport. After the War he returned enthusiastically to Harwich and his beloved 'Summer Lawn'. For all his remarkable wartime contribution he was awarded an unremarkable OBE.

His affection for 'Summer Lawn', which I still own and which he had built, was touching. Perhaps, never having had a real home he was totally absorbed by at last having his own. He remained throughout his life a self-effacing, steely firm and greatly respected man. Never did I hear him swear . . . his favoured expletive being 'bally', than which there can scarcely be more innocuous an oath!

My mother was a contrast. Supremely capable and very outgoing she was the counter-balance to my father and was in the truest sense a 'character'.

For her, living in the peninsular of Harwich was a sacrifice. The Big City of London was her true environment and, although Harwich was then a prosperous port with full employment and local infrastructure, Harwich/Dovercourt had all the character restrictions of an Island Community. It had no hinterland, so anyone who came to Harwich came either to board a ship or to live there . . . no 'through' traffic. The attitudes of its denizens reflected accurately this myopic view of life. Nevertheless my remarkable mother set about her new life – after, I gather, a period of misery and self-doubt, with characteristic vigour. My father's position as the major employer made her the unofficial 'First Lady' of the town and she was a compellingly warm and funny 'Chairperson' of fêtes, St John Ambulance Competitions, Charity Dances and indeed anything else which happened in the Society Agenda of that smallish town. Father's 'out of school' activities involved being Chairman of the Local Magistrates and Chairman of the Harwich Harbour Conservancy Board.

My elder brother, Roy, was very different from me. Very good-looking, with a totally relaxed and easy-going attitude to life (and, it must be recorded, girls) he carried all before him by his effortless charm. He reminded my father of his favourite brother, Ted, who died young. He was very much the apple of my Father's eye; a fact that did not surprise me. I fancy the situation was reversed in my own case in that my mother favoured me.

We had a third brother, Michael, a wonderful looking baby. It is a commentary on how times have changed – particularly in the advance of medicine – that Michael died in 1932 at 12 months from a high temperature generated by pneumonia caught I suspect from brother Roy or myself who had a mild 'flu'. Today of course a baby, however small, rarely dies from such a thing, now that we have all the available drugs for reducing fever. It was a terrible blow for my parents and must have been particularly hard for my mother because with childish four-year old curiosity I kept on asking her for a

Summer Lawn with Dad its proud owner

detailed description of how exactly the Angels had arrived to take Michael away to Jesus, that being the story I was told.

Dovercourt of the early 1930s, the 'posh' residential part of Harwich, remains vivid for me. 'Going down the town' was a daily ritual and that meant having a coffee and gossip in Thompson's Café followed by a leisurely wander round the many family grocers and greengrocers selecting the requirements for a day or two. All were subsequently delivered to the door by errand boys on bikes with their huge baskets forward of the handlebars. Refrigerators – even more than cars – were a rare luxury, so food had to be stored, essentially short term, in the 'pantry'. Shopping was therefore a much more frequent event than today's weekly assaults, car-borne, to a supermarket.

The 'society' of the town, such as it was, consisted of a very large array of maritime-associated worthies. The North Sea ships together with the maintenance 'shops' employed very many people and thus management grades.

It is an interesting contrast to today's high efficiency/high utilization world that so many ships were employed to maintain, for instance, the Harwich/Holland route. The night service Harwich/

Hoek van Holland was maintained by three ships *Vienna, Amsterdam* and *Prague*. They operated on a two weeks on two weeks off rotation and when in service spent each day alongside at either Harwich or the Hoek. The day service Harwich/Vlissingen was operated by Zeeland SM's *Prinses Juliana, Mecklenburg* and *Oranje Nassau* to which the same conditions applied except that the working ships slept (literally!) alongside overnight at Harwich or Vlissingen. Today these services are combined and are maintained by *one* 40 knot high speed ferry Catamaran *Stena Discovery* which makes two round trips per day. Each of the pre-war 14 passenger ships had complete allocated crews despite having every third week 'off'. I still treasure memories of crossing to the Hook c/o the Captain of *Prague*, with my brother Roy. We were given great days out with the van der Roemer and Pieters families.

Then there was Trinity House with up to nine 'tenders' for the Light Authority Service plus crews for the light-ships round the English coast. Trinity House also was responsible for North Sea pilotage, especially for the Thames entrance and river, so all the 'North Channel' pilots were living in Dovercourt and were taken out to the pilot cutter at the Sunk station to wait there for the sequential arrival of ships for London. As the number on board the Sunk station ran down, another 'muster' was called and off to sea went a replenishment load of pilots in the Sturdy *Vigia*.

The ancillary or back-up bodies consisted of seemingly vast numbers of Customs and Immigration officers.

All these, together with the inevitable doctors, dentists etc and local store owners and dignified bank managers and solicitors, added up to a very diverse but interesting body of middle class families.

The road to live in was Fronks Road: and those who resided there had an immutable cachet without further explanation.

I still keep the house in that road where I was born – and spent my early years – and find it incredible to remember that we had *two* maids living in plus a gardener who came in every day. Also we had a nurse when we were very young to augment this impressive staff!

From age seven or so Roy and I became junior members of the Harwich & Dovercourt Parkeston Golf Club. My continuous membership, despite a five-year gap when the course was covered in concrete blocks, tank traps and barbed wire of some 70 years, must set some sort of record.

Both my brother and I started our academic careers at the somewhat grandiosely named 'School of St Francis' or Miss Dunningham's. Miss D was a diminutive figure but a positive genius with her inculcation of knowledge to her group of four to eight year olds, all boys. Miss D clearly was against co-education. My own school reports of those days reveal that I had already developed the idleness and superficiality that I carried throughout my schooldays, but despite that Miss Dunningham somehow drilled into me a level of knowledge which meant that when I went on to my prep school in 1936 at the tender age of eight I was so advanced, as had been brother Roy, as to skip the bottom form and start off with the second years who were one year older.

I have mixed memories of life at Ovingdean Hall. Going back to school was sheer agony, the hated 3.28 train from Victoria to Brighton to me was like a tumbril on the way to the guillotine, and our demeanour over the preceding days must have torn our parents to pieces. When I was 'demobbed' from National Service in the Navy I spent a couple of terms teaching at two prep schools filling in for masters absent for one reason or another. My own experience as a boy plus this latter period as a master has convinced me that boarding for small boys as young as seven and eight can amount almost to cruelty. In the 1930s it was 'the thing to do' and we endured it with not very stiff upper lips. These schools depend so much on the individual Headmaster, and Ovingdean's, the Rev. S.T.E. Chinneck, a former Bradfield House Master who taught Maths (nicknamed Bino after the Binomial theory) was a pompous, humourless and distant man who was totally unsuitable to be put in charge of tiny boys who were already missing the warmth and kindness of their mothers and their homes.

From year to year I lived on a diet of 'could do better' reports, though doing surprisingly well in those subjects that I enjoyed. I have very happy memories of some masters, for instance JEC (a younger Chinneck, who later took over the school from STEC) who unlike his uncle was the perfect prep school master. He exuded discipline (firmly but unlike his uncle equitably applied) and a burning enthusiasm for everything in life. Bee-keeping, bird-watching, butterflies, salmon fishing were all fiendishly entered-into hobbies in which we boys enthusiastically joined.

Then there was J.F. Batsford, a very gentle – I guess today he would be thought rather wet – man who taught music and geography. He was a beautiful pianist and sought manfully to bring on the choir and general appreciation of music and choral singing. He had an easily aroused – though totally futile – temper which we all brutally enjoyed working up.

On the other hand he was a wonderful and kindly man whom we all secretly loved. He composed in 1940, together with John Vaughan, an amusing English master who wrote the libretto, the music for 'Babes in the Wood' a vicious parody on Uncle Adolphus – the villain of the moment – and his gang. The waltz 'There is a splendid star', which I – as the appalling Adolphus – had to sing, still rings in my memory. Another refrain from the show I recall was: 'Too much sauerkraut, too much cheese, he can't touch his toes without bending his knees.' Just which be-medalled Nazi could that have been about?

A thing I learnt during those Ovingdean days was the disadvantage of having siblings at the same school. Inevitably comparisons were always being made between Davis 1 (Roy) and Davis 2 (me). It was not that such comparisons were a matter of envy, it was just that somehow they inhibited one from developing one's own path in one's own way. I came across this phenomenon again with other boys during my brief period of teaching at prep schools after demob from the Navy.

Roy left in 1939 to go on to Felsted and in 1940 a bomb dropped, almost literally on Ovingdean. The fall of France and the imminent prospect of invasion meant that Brighton was no longer the place to be. We were all joyfully sent home while JEC set out to find a country home in a 'safe' area where the school could be re-established. This proved to be Highbullen, at Chittlehamholt near Umberleigh North Devon. It has now become a superior country hotel with a golf course and alleged gourmet cuisine. In 1940 it was a remotely situated house with startlingly beautiful views over the Mole Valley (the home of Henry Williamson's 'Tarka the Otter') and Exmoor.

We had to remove tree stumps in order to produce the semblance of soccer and cricket pitches. As a result our games activities were restricted and other pursuits took their place. We went on extensive cycle rides over the Devon country roads and visited every village church for miles around. The church tower or spire was the only indicator of an imminent village because all road signs had been removed in order to confuse the daily expected parachuted Nazi storm troopers.

Brother Roy and me, c1930

On one such expedition we came across a deserted barn and once inside were startled by the sudden emergence of a beautiful barn owl which scrambled through a hole in the ceiling (clearly the building had once been a small cottage) and flew off, shrieking. Poking our heads through the plaster – I was with Hugh Thomas, now alas prematurely dead from cancer but who became an eminent psychologist – we saw to our surprise and delight some white balls of fluff which were in fact barn owl chicks. We made off with one of them and, with permission and indeed connivance of John Chinneck the Headmaster, made for him a hutch. Food then became a pressing problem and our free time became an endless hunt for rats, mice and other delicacies of the owl menu. In our ignorance we at first cut these up into digestible chunks until one day Charlie – for such was his given name – grabbed a large mouse and proceeded in a series of gulps to swallow it whole, the tail disappearing last.

We had not been aware of the extraordinary digestive system of owls – and other hawks – to gobble an animal and then dispose of

Roy and me and Dusty at Summer Lawn c1934

Sailing on Felicia at Harwich, 1936. Mother is on the right

8

Happy on a ship: RMS Vienna, *1938*

the bones in a neatly encapsulated pellet that is discharged out of its beak. That memorable occasion when Charlie grabbed the mouse convinced us that he was going to expire of massive indigestion, his claws clasping his stomach. On the contrary Charlie grew to full, imposing maturity until the day came for his release. John Chinneck later wrote to me at Bradfield saying that Charlie for months came round most nights wheeling through the dark air and giving a friendly shriek. Bringing him up was a singular and rewarding experience.

All in all Ovingdean was a happy time and I ended up as Head of the School. We followed the progress of the war assiduously, with wall maps and all manner of descriptive literature. We knew every ship in the various Navies, every type of aircraft and every military commander of significance of both sides. We were in our more sombre moments concerned about our parents. My father was at the War office as a Colonel in 'Movements', which meant that both he and my mother were in London staying at the Great Eastern Hotel, Liverpool Street (Room 272 I still recall). With the Blitz occurring nightly – which my brother and I experienced first hand when on school holidays – anything could have happened to any or all of us. Happily it did not. I do however vividly recall looking through our second floor window of the Great Eastern (idiotically through glass) at St Paul's Cathedral majestically silhouetted with fires raging all around it. The survival of that wonderful cathedral was indeed miraculous and it was later saved also from high explosive when a large bomb crashed into the centre aisle and failed to detonate. It was heroically rendered safe by a Major Davis (no relation!) who was properly awarded a George Cross for his effort.

In contrast to the Politically Correct attitudes of a 'New Labour' Britain I suppose we were – though all of us at Ovingdean came from hard working middle-class homes – guilty of considerable puffed-up self esteem. We had occasional clashes with a number of 'evacuees' living with families in villages near to Highbullen. These were never serious and it must be stressed were without exception instigated by them rather than us. They clearly found our accents and attitude extremely offensive and we found their demeanour equally so!

School holidays in the early war years were spent at Dovercourt. It was a protected area and required special passes to reach the town which was dotted with concrete blocks, barbed wire, anti-invasion steel works on the beach (to repel landing craft) – anti-aircraft batteries, barrage balloons and, of course, a significant Naval Base (HMS *Badger*) at Parkeston. The navy presence consisted of destroyers, escorts (the 'Guillemot' class) minesweepers, minelayers and a large MTB/MGB base – HMS *Beehive* – at Felixstowe Dock. A large fleet oiler *War Mehtar* arrived as depot ship to fuel this very considerable fleet. She in turn was replenished every ten days by the smaller *Larchol*.

My very understanding parents allowed me to work on the Pilot Cutter *Landguard* during my holidays where I earned my first money of £2.17s.1d a week . . . including 'danger money'. We had some over-exciting moments including when a collier the *Skagerak* was mined by an acoustic mine (laid from the air) immediately astern of us. The unfortunate pilot, Mr Gardiner, who we had just put on board, was killed in the explosion along with 90 per cent of the crew. In fact the acoustic mines laid by a German seaplane had an extraordinary success, accounting for HMS *Gypsy* and the collier *Swynfleet* as well as the *Skagerak*.

George Smith, the Coxswain of *Landguard*, became my firm friend and I had fun helping him with his daily Log of our activities. He wrote it in most elegant flowing handwriting but – like a PC's report – it was littered with 'Proceeded to . . . (e.g. Sunk lightship)', which overworked verb I presumptuously endeavoured to make him eliminate. He always took it in good heart. Mr Lofts, the quay foreman and Arthur Jennings, a giant boatman with the manners of a high born gentleman all became my dear friends. They all held my father in great awe, but that did not create a barrier to our genuine friendship. It is a tribute to youth, because I do not see myself in any sense a brave person, that during all manner of dangerous wartime experiences I never felt fear. I cannot honestly recall how many occasions the windows of Summer Lawn were blown in, but I certainly well recall seeing a 'Doodle Bug' which had been released from a Dornier 215 and which had not achieved proper altitude, almost literally flying up the road towards our house missing the chimneys by only a few feet. It was a moment of exhilaration, as were the several occasions when we put out incendiary bombs with the extraordinary Government-approved 'Stirrup Pump'.

One also had a grandstand view of Typhoon fighters flying alongside the Doodle Bugs. These fighters discovered accidentally I believe that by tapping the bombs' wings with their own the gyro mechanism they became confused so that the Doodle Bugs dived harmlessly into the sea.

Evenings were very different in those days, without the seductive and all pervading intrusion of television, we listened to the wireless (not radio!), to programmes like ITMA, Happidrome, Garrison Theatre and Forces Favourites plus of course the News Bulletins with those never-to-be forgotten voices of Stuart Hibbard, Alvar Liddell, Bruce Belfrage (who famously continued reading after the briefest of pauses when a bomb hit Broadcasting House) and Frank Phillips. My father, when home, also got great amusement listening to the infamous 'Lord Haw Haw', the egregious William Joyce, starting his propaganda broadcasts with 'Jairmany calling'. I don't remember how many times Haw Haw claimed the sinking of HMS *Ark Royal* before the actual sad event. Incidentally Joyce's execution for 'treason' after the war (when he had long renounced his British Citizenship) was, like many aspects of the Nuremberg War Trials, something which brought no credit on Great Britain.

The next step in life for me was to go on to Bradfield, in autumn 1942. I was fortunate to get into what was unquestionably the 'Cock House' of Bradfield which was 'G' House-on-the-Hill, whose Housemaster was the redoubtable John Moulsdale. John, a former Soccer blue at Cambridge and Welsh Amateur International picked his entrants on the basis of games ability and general 'Strength through Joy' attributes. He was an ardent disciplinarian with a sardonic wit and ruled not by punishments, of which I hardly recall a single example – but by sheer force of personality. The House Prefects were carefully selected and had near God-like power and authority. As a result every member of the House positively *expected* the House to be best in every department, from games through House plays and singing competition to general appearance and discipline. Academic achievement did not seem to intrude to anything like the same extent, but we were not too bad in that area either. My great regret in life has been that whatever my other achievements at Bradfield, I took my studies so lightly. Though an entry Exhibitioner I confined my efforts to an elegant minimum and did just enough to scrape through. John Hills the Headmaster was perceptive indeed in his reports on me during my early years. 'Likes the honours and applause but is unwilling to justify them with really hard work.' 'His reputation for buffoonery will make it hard for him to become an effective school prefect' etc. etc. He was right, though I think the former was harsh following a huge success I had in the Gordon Harker role in our House Play. Despite this I was determined to be Top Dog and I ultimately achieved it.

On the way I was in the Cricket XI (6 for 11 my best bowling analysis, against Tonbridge) Captain of the Football XI, Captain of Rugby Fives and of Squash and in the Athletics Team. I also was Sir Andrew Aguecheek in *Twelfth Night* – with a rave review from W.A. Darlington in *The Times* – and Polonius in *Hamlet*. These productions were in the famous Greek theatre. The first such post-war plays were directed by the incomparable Cecil Bellamy, a housemaster whose real vocation should have been as a Donald Wolfit, whom he definitely resembled. They were marvellous days, those last years at school, and I to this day wonder at how much I crammed into my life. It was just a pity that scholastic work was such an insignificant part of this activity. Tyrone Guthrie suggested that I should enter acting as a career, but that path did not attract me.

1946. Bradfield College Greek Theatre as Polonius in Hamlet

One academic achievement of which I could be reasonably proud was my knowledge of French. At Ovingdean I had been taught by a terrifying spinster, Mlle Peret. We had, I seem to recall, mutual distaste for each other (I was 'lazy', she a harridan in our respective opinions) but she did instil a near perfect French accent. This was improved even at Bradfield by M. Ernest Gabriel Le Grand, a lovely Frenchman with a huge head and splay feet ('Run over by a tank in 1917' was the popular apocryphal story). In his classes one could speak not a word of English for peril of paying 6d *'pour la reconstruction d'Avranches'*, his hometown decimated by the War. *'Je ne comprends pas'* he would respond to an English question.

He did give to me a love of the language, exemplified by the fact

On a public school soccer course at Stamford Bridge in 1945. I am 3rd from left.
Our instructor is the great Walter Winterbottom, later Manager of the England Team

Captain of Bradfield 1st XI (front row, centre), Winter 1946

14

Head of House on the Hill, Bradfield, Summer 1946. I am 5th from left on front row, with John Moulsdale on my left

that I can still quote in full '*Le Loup*' by Alfred de Vigny which he made us learn in 1945.

I scraped my Higher Certificate, also the Entrance Exam to Clare College Cambridge, the latter justifying a State Scholarship. The Headmaster and his delightful wife, Lady Rosemary and his family became great friends and I think JDH (John Hills) ultimately forgave my early trivial demeanour. He always dressed in white tie, black coat and striped trousers – the traditional dress of the Eton 'usher' (whence he came) – and many people, old Boys and contemporary Masters, including I must say my own John Moulsdale, were critical of his snobbery, his thinly disguised impatience with 'lesser' people (including apparently all parents . . . a dangerous antipathy) and so on. Nevertheless I had real admiration and fondness for him, and this despite his early contempt of me. He held the school together and even greatly improved it in those very difficult wartime days when the younger masters were all at War and the school was left with those who were older or who were exempted from War Service for other reasons. Among so many things I shall never fail to be grateful to John Hills for was making me – in his 'Aesthetic Appreciation' class – love Brahms 4th Symphony and the Brothers Van Eyk's *Genter Alterstück*.

It was a tough school, much wedded to 'Privileges,' cold baths and the like, but I have to say none of us really suffered from the harsh regime. There was no bullying – certainly not in my House – nor was there evidence of the famous homosexuality that today's fashion likes to attribute to all boy's public schools. Of course one became almost pathetically ignorant of how to deal with girls. I recall a dance arranged with neighbouring Downe House where my idea of brilliant conversation with a sweet 17-year-old was restricted to describing my astonishing performances on the cricket field and prospects for the forthcoming match against Charterhouse. That match incidentally started wonderfully when we had Charterhouse 17 for 3, after which a near 200 partnership took place between P.B.H. May (112 not out) and A.J. Rimell (91). I choose not to recall my bowling analysis on that afternoon.

On occasion I have made the point that the zenith of any man's career is (or rather was, because the system has changed so much) the period when one is Head of one's School and House. The sheer power and respect that one commanded was heady.

CHAPTER 2

The Royal Navy

T HAT PROUD CONFIDENT feeling of my last days at Bradfield was
brutally destroyed when it came to joining the Royal Navy in
January 1947. I had (naturally) decided that it must be the Senior
Service for me and a disastrous decision that turned out to be. As
Senior Under Officer of the JTC at Bradfield I should have opted for
a 'good' Regiment in the Army, where as an officer I might have
done something useful and honed my management skills. Contemporaries of mine served for instance in Malaysia or Palestine or Africa.
My lot was however to join the RN at Cookham in Wiltshire in
January 1947 on perhaps the coldest day of the coldest winter of the
century. As we were marched off the train at Corsham, wet, hungry,
cold and thoroughly miserable with foreboding, the cries of 'You'll
be sorry!' from hardened veterans of two weeks' service rang in our
near-frozen ears. The typically inefficient Naval Shore station HMS
Royal Arthur, ably abetted by the Labour Government Ministry of
Fuel, had succeeded in totally running out of coal, which meant that
we had to sleep in unheated Nissen huts. My first heavy responsibility
as Class Leader was to take a party out on a lorry to find a coal dump
and load ten tons onto our open vehicle. Since the coal was frozen
solid one had to more-or-less 'mine' it once again with inadequate
pick-axes. Having Lieutenant Philip Mountbatten as a nearby
Divisional officer gave a certain cachet to the camp, but no comfort
from the cold and living conditions.

The Navy in 1947 was in a pretty run-down state, both
mechanically and mentally. The War was won, the country was
predictably tired of the armed forces and all that they represented, and
there seemed very little point or objective for the forces to aim at.
The regulars, weary of training National Servicemen who came and
went, showed their contempt for this ill-disciplined procession or
'shower' of dispirited and disoriented young men.

I shall never forget the hopelessness one felt. After kitting out and
initial training at *Royal Arthur*, we were shipped in an unheated train
on a five-hour cross-country ride up to Warrington Lancashire where

at HMS *Gosling* we were to be turned into a group of highly trained razor-sharp seamen . . . or something.

HMS *Gosling* was at least an efficient and disciplined station and for the second time I was made Class Leader of my Class. This position entailed considerable responsibility for the Class, behaviour, living quarters etc etc. Class Leaders wore an armband but other than that were rewarded with neither pay nor official rank. Authority could be achieved only by force of personality and persuasion because there were no practicable sanctions one could employ over one's peers with whom one lived, ate, trained and slept. In other words it was a thankless task, and ill-conceived by those in authority. However, one survived, and I made some good 'mates', but this was because they were a most likeable lot of fellow-sufferers, ranging from Hull fishermen to Welsh GWR firemen. One singular achievement at *Gosling* was a day when we, on a boat-pulling exercise, actually succeeded in getting shipwrecked on a colliery 'flash'. We were remarkably inefficient at pulling on those heavy oars (sweeps) and in the confusion we were driven ashore by a sprightly breeze and our cutter was holed and ignominiously sank.

A trivial yet poignant ending to my time at HMS *Gosling* was at a dance on the final night. There were some very pretty Wrens present, one of whom I had admired throughout the months of training . . . but, Public School trained, I had never approached her because we had not been introduced! On that evening 'Taffy' my Welsh railway fireman friend dragged her across the floor to me saying 'Here Cynthia, you must meet my friend Jim who thinks you're smashing!' Initially overcome with confusion we proceeded to have a delightful evening.

The very next morning I was drafted from Warrington down to the RN Signals School at Chatham. This little cameo certainly illustrates what inarticulate clots the Public School system could produce, certainly in their relationship with girls. My four-hour long 'romance' with Cynthia devolved into the exchange of a couple of letters and sudden death.

Since I was designated to the Signals Branch, training became specialized and so did one's fellow National Servicemen. Instead of the rough but uncomplicated trainee seamen and stokers, we were a group of former blue-collar bank clerks, Post Office clerks and the like who seemed up to their necks in class prejudice and a smart alec

Class Leader at HMS Gosling, *1947. (I am 4th from left, front row)*

attitude . . . at least that was the general attitude that they applied to me. Once again I was the reluctant Class Leader and the Class generally did their best to make the carrying out of this difficult duty as fraught as possible. It is a commentary on my life experience up till those Navy years that until then I had had literally no experience of the type of fellow citizen that I was to meet, in such cramped conditions in the 'Andrew' . . . as the RN was unlovingly called on the lower deck. Very many could only just read. The *Daily Mirror* and Sunday *News of the World* constituted the staple literature diet, augmented, astonishingly, by children's comics. Communication of the verbal kind was of course affected by this. 'F__K'/'F_____G' punctuated most words in every sentence and it was impossible to have a logical debate or discussion on almost any topic (with the possible exception of football).

This sounds a sweeping generalization but, in my experience, was sadly true. How, one might ask, can one discuss any matter in any depth when one's vocabulary is limited to some 60 words or fewer? Inductive or deductive argument is beyond an individual with such limitations. I became the scribe for the earlier units at *Royal Arthur* and *Gosling*. It was fascinating writing grandiose love-letters to girl friends. I tended – on instruction – to make the letters treacly romantic and full of gushing protestations of love, and was rewarded by being shown the replies, 'Ern, you've got to be real romantic!' was one such.

The cheerful ignorance was however replaced at Chatham by a veneer of learning and wearisome political correctness that in some ways was more difficult to handle. I am sure I sound priggish and smug in these paragraphs but I have to say that I tried my level best to integrate but was usually rebuffed by a mindless prejudice against someone who they labelled a Silver-Spooned Public School Toff. The label was attached instantly. I found that the very best notably unprejudiced shipmates were from Newcastle and lads from Humberside and Yorkshire/Lancashire. The trickiest by far were the Cockneys.

At Chatham (Borstal actually, because that School of Learning/ Correction was next door, the other side of a barbed wire fence) we were trained to become 'Trained Operator' telegraphists and signallers . . . We learned Morse to a remarkable speed, Morse-typing (straight onto a typewriter) and basic, very basic, Radio Maintenance.

The Morse Code is something that lives with one forever and I find myself even today admiring such charming words as Aerial and Beef Essence, on which we used to practise our keying ability. Like riding a bike it is something one never forgets, or more accurately in terms of the Morse Code, one is stuck with!

Happily there was opportunity to indulge in some sport at Chatham and I earned a modicum of grudging respect by winning the Nore Command High Hurdles Championship and also playing for the 'Ship' at soccer and cricket.

To escape from the claustrophobic atmosphere of living 30 in one Nissan hut I occasionally spent a night in a Salvation Army hostel in Rochester. The sheer bliss of sleeping between sheets in a silent room free of expletive-filled mindless talk was an unspeakable joy.

Training came to an end and one then awaited one's draft to a ship. Mine proved to be to RML 512 in Londonderry. The draft assembled in Chatham Barracks and four or five of us were put under the temporary command of Stoker 'Dickie' Bailey who was also destined for my ship.

Dickie was chosen because he had sewed on his uniform the badge of a Stoker Mechanic . . . to which he was completely unentitled but

Roy was already a Sub Lt RNVR so I had to salute him!
With Dad at Summer Lawn, 1947

which ostensibly conferred on him a certain seniority over the rest of us. Also he was a Regular while we were press-ganged National Servicemen. On that journey via Euston and Heysham/Belfast, as our leader and later as a shipmate, Dickie – from Charlton – proved the most arrestingly clueless person I have ever met. It was amazing that under his 'command' we did not end up in Aberdeen or Penzance. My introduction to Londonderry and RML512 was not encouraging. Already the city was simmering, though not yet actually erupting, which came about decades later when Miss Bernadette Devlin started pulling up paving stones. Its cheerless atmosphere of run-downness unemployment and indifferent weather was depressing. RML512, commanded by lanky, uncharismatic Lieutenant Eric B, bore all the characteristics of its commanding officer. We used to operate with the 4th Escort Flotilla, the destroyers *Crispin* and *Creole* the Frigates *Loch Arkaig Loch Tralaig* and *Loch Veyatie*, together with various submarines including *Aurochs* and *Alliance*. We also with RML 515, were the mail-boats and stores carriers to the flotilla when they were moored off Moville at the entrance to Lough Foyle. 1948 was a beautiful summer, and together with the PO motor mechanic of our vessel I had the occasional good run ashore. Through going to evensong at St Columba's Cathedral we struck up a friendship with the Dean of Derry, a kindly Pickwickian character with a nice wife who used to ask us round for various meals. As we were allowed ashore in plain clothes (aka 'civvies') it was amusing to have an officer from another ship as a fellow guest who became most confused when he discovered he was unwittingly breaking bread with members of the lower deck. Wearing uniform, bell-bottoms, rapidly made one aware of the rigid class distinction or no-go areas that existed for the Other Ranks. It was quite inappropriate for instance to endeavour to go out to dinner at one of the smarter hotels . . . not that I could have afforded it. Incidentally living conditions aboard an RML were mostly appalling. Ten people living, eating, sleeping in a tiny fo'c'sle was a very wearing experience. There was no escape from the incessant vacuous conversation and general noise.

My final posting in the King's Navy was as a Watchkeeper in the 'Citadel', that concrete edifice behind Admiralty Arch. It was the land-based nerve centre of RN Broadcasts and was manned 24 hours a day. It meant a virtual home life . . . I stayed with an aunt and uncle in South London . . . which was a considerable relief and gentle preparation for demobilization which blessedly came about in February 1949. Much has been written since about National Service, its benefits and it defects. My own reflection is that in general the Army and possibly the Air Force handled it reasonably well. The Navy, however, had not the slightest idea nor plan to deal with their unhappy unwelcome recruits and blocked any possible route to promotion. *No* officer training or promotional prospects were available or offered during my Naval Career and morale in general was at a pathetically low level. In later years I have made friends with numerous (six to be precise) First Sea Lords plus many Admirals, all but one of whom have been younger than I. I have not revealed to them the genuine disappointed sadness I had for the RN in the late 1940s. The Senior Service certainly let itself down in its man management in those days. I should perhaps balance this criticism by saying that I have for the past 30 years lectured to the RN officers at the Staff College (now the Joint Services Staff College) and to the Lieutenants' Course. The professionalism and dedication of these (admittedly 'upwardly mobile') officers, mostly of Commander and Lt Commander rank, is enormously impressive. It is sad only that their prospects are becoming increasingly narrow with the constant diminution of the seagoing fleet.

My 'demob' came early in 1949 so that I had some ten months ahead of me before going up to Clare Cambridge in October.

It was the end of a melancholy period of service. For all my life I had positively worshipped the Royal Navy and wanted to go to Dartmouth and spend my life as a Regular Officer. My father had gently suggested that it might be better to go to a regular Public School and consider 'Special Entry' to the RN at age 18. He felt it was inadvisable to narrow one's options at the early age of 13. He was, as usual, right.

CHAPTER 3

The approach to Cambridge

WHAT NOW TO DO in order to prepare for an Academic life and shake off the torpor and aimlessness of the peacetime Navy? At that time I visited Bradfield and the Headmaster, still John Hills, suggested that I would enjoy teaching for a couple of terms at a preparatory school.

I took up this suggestion and quickly found myself at Wellingborough preparatory school, deputizing at very short notice for the Second Master who had been taken ill.

The School, adjacent to the Public School and part of it, was headed by Robert Britten, the older brother of Benjamin Britten. It was about 50:50 boarding:day boys and the boys came from Wellingborough itself or neighbouring Northampton. All the famous names of that shoe manufacturing town were represented, e.g. Willie Barker plus John the son of the Saxby family of Wellingborough who make those succulent Pork Pies. Anne Saxby was Robert Britten's secretary and she, her sister Joey and indeed the whole family became life long friends. They certainly brightened my life and I thoroughly enjoyed the whole term there teaching and, of course, coaching games with those bright Midlands boys. The aura of enthusiasm was the precise antidote to the gloomy sloth of the 1948 Navy.

The absent Deputy Head returned for the following term, happily fully restored, so I had to move on. I recall an interesting economic fact in that at the conclusion of my Wellingborough term I decided to ask the Saxby girls, with brother Roy to make up the four, out to Dinner in London. We went to the Edmundo Ros Club for a Dinner/Dance and the evening absorbed my entire wages for the half-term at Wellingborough. It was not however too startling an amount (certainly not in today's values), being £27.50!

The prep school teaching proved a useful – if not very remunerative – way of spending time before going to Cambridge in October, so I put my name down with the Secretary of the IAPS (the Incorporated Association of Preparatory Schools) for a further possible term. This bore fruit and off I went to Hydneye House in Hastings.

It was a nicely situated school with two wildly different Joint Head Masters. Mr Maltby was a large somewhat challenging man immensely proud of having been an Oxford Hockey Blue (whose blazer and Vincent's tie he wore at every opportunity), while Mr Tanner was a most mild and gentlemanly sort rather overwhelmed by his colleague. Tanner was however a beautiful games player, a genuine 'natural' with effortless skills at tennis and cricket.

I enjoyed a very sunny summer term there. The boys were an amusing lot, all from well-to-do middle class families. A feature which disturbed me at the time was the very high proportion of boys whose parents had divorced. Then, even more than today, money made separation easy and boarding schools provided the answer for the children whose homes had broken up. Allison Attlee, daughter of the then Prime Minister, was an Under Matron with another girl whose name I forget. but generally there was drastic shortage of feminine company. Also Hastings itself was not to me a very agreeable town.

At the end of the term Mr Tanner asked me if I had some capital with a view to buying him out after Cambridge. I stammered my appreciation of this offer, though (even ignoring my capital deficiency) I never really considered taking it up. Even then I recognized a certain degree of truth in George Bernard Shaw's aphorism describing schoolmasters 'Men among boys, boys among men'. I had thoroughly enjoyed this teaching interlude and the refreshing experience of being with the young unprejudiced enquiring minds of teen-age boys, in such contrast with the closed frighteningly ignorant minds of those I had lived with on the lower deck of the Royal Navy. However it was novelty, both to me and to the boys, that made me such a success. But that would not have lasted . . . and in any case I had my 'ships' to think about. This sounds like a blanket criticism of schoolmasters. It is not meant to be, though I have long held the view that to be a perfect teacher one should always have had life experience outside the academic world. Obviously not always practical however.

After the end of term I enjoyed my first post-war grown-up experience of overseas travel. I went with my parents on a prolonged trip, courtesy of DFDS, about which more later, to Denmark, Norway and Sweden. I had a great time, particularly in Copenhagen where I met an amusing crowd of young Danes, with whom to share evenings of dancing, singing and the rest in the Scarlet Pimpernel Tavern, and related hostelries. It initiated an affection for Denmark that has lasted.

Another hobby that has persisted has been my love of drawing. In the days before television, and particularly during the war years, evenings were spent listening to the radio, to the News of course but also to the contemporary shows like ITMA, Garrison Theatre, Variety Band Box, the Happidrome and, conspicuously, the Brains Trust whose regulars were Professor Joad, Dennis Brogan, Julian Huxley, and Commander Campbell (a 'sea dog' who actually was a Paymaster Supply officer) whose every answer was prefixed by 'when I was in Patagonia, Tristan da Cunha . . .' etc etc, in contrast to the precise Joad's 'It depends what you mean by . . .' Radio unlike TV did give one the chance to do something else while listening and I spent happy evenings producing all manner of drawings, mostly maritime scenes but also animals, birds, and other flora and fauna. I now wish I had had formal artistic training, but I maintain the habit by drawing throughout the many conferences and Board meetings which are a feature of my life. At school this habit was severely criticized on the basis that I was 'not attending'. The reverse is however the case in that drawing prevents my butterfly mind from straying and I can always recall what was being said by looking at the feature I was sketching at the time.

Incidentally, once the war was over my father was allowed to return to Harwich to resume his position as Boss of now British Rail shipping services. During the six years he had been released from the Royal Engineers as a Colonel and transferred to the Ministry of War Transport as Assistant Director of Sea Transport. His last main job there was to assemble the smaller merchant ships for the Normandy Landings. He was awarded an OBE for this, which, in my opinion, was a less than adequate honour for all that he had achieved.

In October 1949 came the day to go up to Clare College Cambridge. In those days it was a delightful place to be. The Master, Sir Henry Thirkill, was a wonderful man. He knew the name of every member of the college and exuded courtesy and charm. By today's norms he was gloriously politically incorrect and virtually selected for Clare only those who he felt would blend easily into the ethos of the College. I was fortunate in being awarded a State

Dad, around 1950

Scholarship but even so had to undergo a specific College entrance exam and interviews with 'Thirks'. He was totally understanding, indeed he needed to be because brother Roy had preceded me. Thirks had warm memories of brother Roy. At Clare Roy had studied Engineering which subject he totally loathed (he switched later to medicine and ended as a consultant anaesthetist), but he had otherwise led a spectacular student life with the result that in one Tripos exam he actually scored 'zero'. He did ultimately achieve his Engineering Degree and served a period in the RN as 'Senior' Engineer in the destroyer *Wakeful* and cruiser *Ceylon*. A distinguished rugby player at Felsted he had found more intriguing activities at university and played but one game in three years, not for Clare but I believe Jesus College with his friend Micky Steele-Bodger.

Cambridge was a specially interesting place in 1949. The undergraduates had all, with the exception of the medical students, been in the forces either during the War or doing National Service. There were many who had seen considerable action.

Graduation at Cambridge with two great friends, Dick DuCann (later QC) and Geoff Weston DSC, former 1st Lieut of HMS Amethyst. *Both, alas, now dead*

Dick DuCann my great friend who later became a distinguished QC and criminal barrister had been in the Palestine Police at a time when there was a most unpleasant guerrilla war being fought between the Palestinians and the emergent Israel. Another of my year was Geoff Weston who had been awarded a DSC as 1st Lieutenant of *Amethyst* in the famous Yangtse Incident.

This 'maturity' manifested itself in the area of sport. Those of us who might have thought we had an outside chance of gaining a 'Blue' were in those days confronted with awesome competition. For instance in my first year the Cambridge Cricket Team batting order was: Dewes, Sheppard, Doggart, May, all Test players and they were followed by others who had almost without exception gained their County Cap. *Both* varsity Rugger Teams went to Twickenham one year undefeated . . . a unique event.

I think we were a fairly disciplined bunch. There was the inevitable frivolity but University rules and the authority of the Procters and 'Bulldogs' was never challenged. This attitude seems in stark contrast to today's beliefs where in so many instances – not just among students – the breaking of a custom or law is deemed not to be the fault of the transgressor but is due more to the stupidity or irrelevance of the customs or laws themselves.

The Cambridge 'Footlights' were beginning to gain universal acclaim with such names as Julian Slade (of inter alia *Salad Days* fame) Simon Phipps, Simon Raven etc.

One certainly made some great friends. Among the most exceptional in my own case was Jim English (more correctly James Fairfield English Jr). He was a Mellon Fellow – named after Paul Mellon who had enjoyed a memorable period at Clare following Berkeley College Yale and who had established two-year exchanges – and came from Hartford Connecticut where his father was Anglican Bishop. Despite the fact that he existed on a totally superior intellectual plane from myself we became great friends and I shall never forget my first trip to Paris that I made with him. One must recall that the War had precluded *any* overseas trips for 6 long years and when we at last were permitted to go each UK citizen had the princely *annual* exchange allowance of £25. It is amazing what we achieved on that.

Jim was a most organized tourist. Each day he produced a list of those sights that we had to see . . . everything from the Louvre and Jeu de Paumes to Les Invalides and every conceivable Church in that great City. My naiveté was exposed when we were drinking absinthe – or something equally appropriate – in Le Librairie on the left Bank in company with, among others, Jean Paul Sartre. I was having an animated conversation with an attractive blonde. Jim leant across and said 'James, before you get too involved with that girl, I should warn you that She's a fellah!'

The days were thus spent on 'Culture with a Capital K' and the evenings in James's words 'Doing the things that *you* like'. Thus the Crazy Horse, the Moulin Rouge, the Folies Bergères and other locals less salubrious were enthusiastically visited.

But in term time I am not quite sure how much I really achieved. I played a lot of games – up to Varsity *second* team standard (e.g. the Falcons Football XI, the 'Sparrows' Rugby fives team etc. etc.) and enjoyed it. I also became Secretary of the Clare JCR, a post entailing being the link between undergraduates and the Fellows and staff generally. I emerged after three agreeable years with second class Honours in Law and Economics (the latter proving to be most decidedly Jeremy Benthams's 'Dismal Science' . . . at least to me). Though never wanting to be a practising barrister, I enjoyed Law.

I found that to achieve even a Second required a quality of study and effort that I had never before put in. It was the ultimate penalty I had to pay for my idleness at Bradfield.

Socially Cambridge was enjoyable. There were far fewer under-graduettes in those days but I was much blessed by having some wonderful girl friends during those years; one Swiss (their national swimming champion); one Danish (very gentle and beautiful); one Swedish and one Dutch. Perhaps a sign of things to come?

Already in my last year I had made up my mind that what I wanted was a career in Shipping, so I went along to see Mr Sinker at the Cambridge University Appointments Board with that clear objective in mind. He was most kind and supportive but said graduate opportunities in the great shipping companies were few and far between. There was one notable exception. 'P&O take an occasional graduate but there is usually a positive queue of applicants,' he warned. However I persisted and my application went in and, to my delight, I was invited to an interview at P&O's HQ, 122 Leadenhall Street, during the Easter Vacation. The interview was impressive being conducted by Mr (later Sir) Donald Anderson and Lord Simon, the two Deputy Chairmen of the Group, supported by egregious and rather gloomy general manager Wilfred Mizen. I was put totally at my ease in very grand surroundings and even offered a cigarette by Donald Anderson. (Everyone smoked in those days and 'Duty Frees' in the RN had fuelled my taste for cigarettes.) At one stage I was asked what I was doing in the Easter Vacation and I confessed that I was going to Leiden University in Holland to do a course in International Comparative Law. 'Why, is that your speciality?' asked Sir Donald, and I had to confess that it certainly was not, but I thought the venture could be a lot of fun, considering the Cambridge colleagues of mine who were going. Immediately I had said it I thought what a brainless frivolous answer I had given. The impression I had made on them, I felt, would not be that of a serious, solid committed possible employee. 'Oh well,' I thought, 'that's probably that and at any rate it had been a very pleasant chat with those great men' . . . and off I went to Leiden, to enjoy the Student Corps Sociëteit 'Minerva', drink large quantities of beer and jonge genever, take part in 'Moots' (mock trials) and meet some very nice people – men, and, predictably, girls. Dick DuCann and I somehow became the major participants in all the legal activities but, even more physically demanding, in the out-of-school goings-on. An interesting sequel many years later was meeting one of our most active Dutch sparring partners from Leiden when he was the Netherlands Ambassador in London. It was an instant bond!

On return from Holland there was the nice surprise awaiting me in the shape of a letter from Wilfred Mizen offering me a place as a P&O 'Learner'. Ironically by the same post came a similar letter from Cunard to whom I had also made an approach – it was a dizzy feeling being given the chance actually to choose between the two great shipping groups. In fact it was not so difficult to decide since, despite the aura of the 'Queens' and the Trans-Atlantic route, P&O seemed to me far more attractive with its exotic history and its unequalled number of routes. 'The Merchant Navy, the Royal Navy and the P&O' in ascending order of precedence was a self-appreciating phrase already known to me!

CHAPTER 4

P&O

THUS IN OCTOBER 1952 I arrived again at 122 Leadenhall Street and somewhat apprehensively crossed the courtyard, with its turntable to cope with the lorries that carried in the bullion, and reported to the correspondence department and its delightful if somewhat vague Deputy Head Harold Duncombe. His loyalty to the company was total, and indeed infectious, and he emphasized the enormous opportunity I had been accorded and enjoined me to learn everything I could and 'grasp this wonderful chance'. On my side I was more than happy to do just that. The twelve months that followed were spent in all the significant departments of the company: Export Freight (including the monumentally boring task of 'bill passing' i.e. matching the mates receipts with the Bills of Lading, which latter immediately became legal marketable instruments and documents of title), working in the Royal Docks and Tilbury, the Cargo Claims Department, the Import Freight, the Passenger Department – in Cockspur Street, etc etc etc. The emphasis certainly was on 'Learning' which meant finding out how P&O did things and then going forward and doing likewise. I was definitely not encouraged nor expected to question what I found . . . just *learn*. Nevertheless I enjoyed it all.

The experience in the Docks was illuminating. Two things in particular struck me. First, in regard to the actual dockworkers. There were two unions involved, the TGWU and the ASD (stevedores and dockers) whose agendas frequently did not coincide. It was hardly surprising that each felt aggrieved at the treatment they were accorded by the employers. There were no 'pithead baths' in which to clean up after work before trudging home over the cobbled streets. The 'Mobile', a rather ancient van, which served tea, coffee and such as buns and sandwiches rolled up twice a day on the quayside when work stopped for refreshment. If it was raining it was not very agreeable and of course rain immediately stopped work and hatch tents were unfurled while the men played a hand or two of cards. The 'employers' were not really the shipping companies but were stevedoring companies to whom the work was contracted. The largest (and P&O's contractor) was Scruttons. The men were picked up daily on the 'Stones' and understandably felt themselves to be casual labour treated not unlike cattle . . . with similar life quality. It was to me hardly surprising that labour relations were continually hostile and created an unofficial champion of the men, an orator of some brilliance, in the person of the Jack Dash. Each morning with few exceptions he also was on the stones intoning 'Good morning, brothers' (the title he chose for his autobiography) and exhorting the men to take action against the latest injustice, real or imagined. It was an act that the men thoroughly enjoyed, but which over the years cost shipowners literally millions of pounds in lost time and ultimately cost dockers their jobs.

One day I was standing alongside a hatch acting as a 'checker' when a docker looked up from the 'tween deck and said 'Who's that b____d?' and Jack rejoined 'Oh it's one of them f____g Student Princes'. The name stuck.

Second, it was quite astonishing that the shipowners, who were paying very large sums of money for better, faster, smarter ships, did not invest at least a fraction of that money in improving the port facilities. On the contrary this was left to the PLA (the Port of London Authority) who did little or nothing. Overhead cranes in the warehouses were left inoperative and rusting while the cargo was slowly handled manually. The warehouses themselves were ineffic-ient with stanchions and pillars clogging the floor space and hindering movement. The roadways meanwhile became a motionless traffic jam of lorries. The consequence was that these sleek cargo liners which had rushed the consignments across thousands of miles of ocean at high speed (P&O already in 1951 had 22-knot ships) spent up to 50 per cent of their time in port. The cargo equally spent days, weeks, even months before it was 'cleared' and sent on its way to the consignee.

Pilferage was pretty rife and damage all too common. I recall after the Coronation ceremony in 1953 a Maharajah's beautiful new Rolls Royce being shipped back to India. It was stowed in the square of the hatch so as to avoid scratching by excessive handling in the hold. This was a splendid precaution but which failed in its objective somewhat when a steel hatch beam detached itself from a crane and fell arrow-like down the hatch and through the roof and floor of the superb vehicle. A rather large claim resulted accompanied by much loss of face.

I cannot speak with enough affection of the people I met during my prolonged 'Docks period'. The dockworkers themselves rejoiced in such names as 'Tiger' Orchard. They were amusing rascals and had much justification for their feeling of somehow being outside any form of caring employment. The P&O staff were devoted servants frequently working long hours of unpaid overtime in order to get a ship away. Their only 'bunce' was just a glass (or two) of whisky with the Cargo Officer on board before sailing. My journey from and to Gloucester Road via District Line to East Ham thence by bus to the 'Harland Gate' took a good hour and a half and I arrived back tired and unwashed. I truly felt a real fellowship with my dock colleagues. P&O itself inspired a deep loyalty. Every employee felt part of a family of which we were hugely proud. Pay was generally very poor (I started at £450 a year and this took a painfully long time to rise to a living wage). However the award of a Christmas turkey and mini-hamper was sensed as very adequate compensation from our magnificent company. I might mention that many years later in 1972 during the sad one-year Chairmanship of Ford Geddes a combination of the efforts of McKinsey and Hay-MSL succeeded in their ham-fisted search for 'efficiency' virtually destroying the old espirit de corps and company affection in a matter of weeks. That however came about some twenty years after my docks period.

After the docks the 'Learning' continued with periods spent in every department of Head Office. Accounts, Cargo Claims, Export and Import Freight (Curiously each Freight Department had its own Manager and the two bickered incessantly over the routing of the cargo ships on their 'coastal' itinerary), Passenger Department in Cockspur Street and so on.

Being a Learner/'Student Prince' was rather a strange existence. On the one hand it was hugely privileged to be on a very high speed 'Fast Track' but there were predictable pressures at working alongside highly intelligent colleagues who knew that they were not. I must say however that I was shown nothing but kindness as I progressed through the departments and made some very good friends. This state of affairs replicated itself when on secondment to the Agencies (Mackinnon Mackenzie which via BI (British India) was a subsidiary of the P&OSN Co.). I must say that my experience of overt jealousy and hostility was minimal, which in a way was surprising. Jealousy did however reveal itself many years later, as I shall reveal.

The year in London came to an end in the summer of 1953 and as a family we went down to the Palace Hotel in Torquay for a form of 'embarkation leave'. I knew that I was to be despatched to the Far East for a minimum of four years. I mention this holiday at this, then lovely, hotel because it had a considerable affect on my morale over the next years. The Palace is marvellously situated adjacent to Babbacombe Cove and has its own nine-hole pitch and putt golf course, some ten tennis courts including three matchless indoor ones plus squash and other excellent facilities. Those who came were mostly families with their teen-age to mid-twenties sons and daughters. We always had a marvellous time there but on that occasion there was a special in that I fell hopelessly in love (reciprocated) with a beautiful girl. She was studying Speech Therapy and lived normally in Cheshire. It went at whirlwind pace and she later came down to Harwich whence we went across to Holland (*with my mother, such was the regimen of those days*) on an idyllic few days seeing that country. Then we parted and I sailed off shortly afterwards in the 10-knot BI general cargo ship *Landaura*. Up to that time I had never experienced such heartache as that parting. There I was leaving Father and Mother and Brother all my friends and lovely Annette for a minimum of four years.

P&O, in the shape of Wilfred Mizen, had decided that the way to extract most benefit from the voyage was to travel in a cargo vessel. but why, I was constantly asking myself, *this* one. Her schedule was meandering: Genoa, Port Said, Suez, Port Sudan, Aden, Colombo, Madras 'Vizag', and ultimately Calcutta. We were overtaken by every other ship. Captain 'Abie' Andrew was generally mildly drunk and pretty incomprehensible even when not, the Chief Officer was a dour Scot, the Chief Engineer was very companionable but decidedly boring, while the Chief Steward, a Mr Brownless from Hartlepool, made extremely heavy weather of possibly the least demanding job in nautical history. My fellow passenger was Walter Kerr, a recently inducted 'Learner', not from University but the son of Walter Kerr Senior, the Secretary of the BI Company who had approached Sir William Currie the P&O Chairman asking if a chance could be given for his son. Walter was a stolid friendly but by no means stimulating soul. The previous winter he had gained a solitary cap as 2nd Row forward for Scotland in the Calcutta Cup match where the Scots had been systematically thrashed by England. Looking back at the voyage I remain amazed at how I retained my sanity. Of course the ports were new to me and interesting. I recall going ashore with Walter in Port Sudan impeccably dressed, to have a drink in the Red Sea Hotel watched by amused 'Fuzzy Wuzzies' who were working the ship. The amusement was caused by our dress because none in the expat community in that unbearably hot place ever wore anything other than shorts and short-sleeved shirt.

In face of the sentence of four/five years away and what and whom I had left behind the long days at sea became a kind of mental torture. Ultimately we reached Calcutta. The unique smell of India had assailed the ship some two weeks before when we were yet in the Indian Ocean but when we berthed in Kidderpore Dock in Calcutta the extraordinary mix of people swarming like flies (accompanied by cows, rickshaws, open buses, trams with passengers clinging to the outside of roofs, 'pie-dogs'), and the noise hit me like a sledge-hammer. How on earth could I survive living in this bedlam? Spirits were somewhat relieved when we arrived at the Chummery where Walter and I were to live with three other Assistants (as we were all called).

The Chummery, situated in Lord Sinha Road was in fact a beautiful house with marble floors and interior walls, set back from the road with its own tennis court. From my spacious first-floor sitting room/bedroom I could see from the balcony a pair of King Vultures happily nesting. I was already allocated a 'bearer' (servant) called Sita Ram who I inherited from my predecessor Learner, Peter Parry. Sita Ram set about looking after me and my belongings directly he set eyes on me, and with the enthusiasm so typical of Indian servants. One day we five bachelors in the Chummery decided to have a group picture taken of our staff with their dependants. The total was 160 (!) who relied on our wages to survive. There were all the categories, Bearer (personal servant), Borchi (cook), Sweeper (very low caste, poor chap, who did the floors), Mahli (gardener), Dirwans (Gurkha types responsible with their kukris – razor sharp swords – for night time security) Dhobis (washing) and so on. All had big families so the number was not surprising.

The Head Office of Mackinnons was situated virtually on the site of the 'Black Hole' of Calcutta. It was a very large and at that time

With Sita Ram and the 'moti' (washer-up!)

non-air-conditioned edifice cooled – if that be the word – by huge overhead punkahs (slow revolving stir-about fans) which were not sufficiently effective to counteract the fact that papers on one's desk tended to stick to one's forearm as you worked.

An early visit to the Company Doctor, 'Tubby' Garrow was advised so I dutifully trooped along to see him. His recommendations were never to be forgotten. 'What are your drinking habits, Jim?' he asked, to which I stumblingly replied that I liked the occasional glass of beer. 'No damn' good,' said Dr Garrow. 'To survive in this place you need three or four chota pegs (small whiskies) a night.' The prescription proved an effective one, because it was noticeable that another totally abstemious young Assistant, the son of a clergyman, was regularly down with Calcutta Tummy, while we the steady adherents of 'Tubby's prophylactic' were rarely so infected.

The traditional 'cold weather' was quickly upon us and represented a very pleasant time in Calcutta. The temperature is a delightful 70–80°F and the sun shines. Also it is the time when all the wives remain in Town *plus* the 'cold weather girls'. The latter, mostly daughters of the local burrah sahibs, tended to leave again for home when the hot weather started in March. In these circumstances

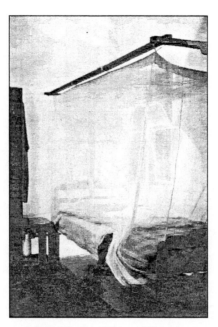

My bed in the Calcutta Chummery

Calcutta in winter had a vibrant social atmosphere with many parties, dances (the 'Vingt-et-un' – laid on by 21 bachelors, was a spectacular one) and the rest. At an early such function I had the good luck to meet a most beautiful and sweet daughter of a retired burrah sahib – who was out for the season. The short result was that we spent every available moment together, playing tennis or golf, going out to dinner etc etc. This sounds perfidious behaviour on my part in view of the girl I had left behind but I conscientiously wrote home to her and confessed to the turmoil in which I then found myself. Indeed it was terrible because in a space of months I had met, and fallen for, two of the most wonderful girls I had yet met. When Shirley Ann sailed for home in March I saw her off from a dark Kidderpore Dock in the Ellerman *City of Chester.*

I felt dreadful and remember saying as I left 'Stay there at the top of the gangway until I reach the corner of the go-down and we will wave, and then please go to your cabin and sleep'. I shall always remember that moment, and quite literally I felt that the bottom had fallen out of my life . . . and Calcutta was very different thereafter.

Life of course had to go on and I threw myself into work which in my case was as 'E2' (number 2 in the extra steamers – i.e. non liner-department of Mackinnon Mackenzie as Managing Agents of

A tennis afternoon at the 'Chummery', Calcutta, in 1954. Shirley Ann is on my right

the BISNCO). The weather became ghastly, hot and humid, so that daily ship visits and voyage committees could only be held at 6.00 a.m. before the sun gained its sizzling heat. The BI of course did not have air-conditioning on the ships – too namby pamby perhaps? Or was it because the company naval architects did their work in the chilly parts of England and Scotland? Either way the 10–12 knot BI cargo 'liners' made an interesting contrast to their sleek 18-knot counterparts operated by Hoëgh and Hansa with their advanced cargo gear and cool air-conditioned accommodation.

Voyage committees were enlivened by the performance of the BI Marine Superintendent Donald Lattin and Engineer Superintendent George Cruickshank who shared a capacious house which they labelled 'Hangover House'. Having described himself as feeling 'like a bunch of broken springs' George usually proceeded to demolish any hapless Chief Engineer who raised a material matter of concern with the words 'Aye, that's enough of that. It's a purely Departmental matter'. After that discussion would melt away and the Chief Engineer would say not a word thereafter.

Communication with the 'owners' in London was customarily by a weekly 'Secretary's Letter' to which all Departments contributed their paragraphs which were cobbled together by E2 (me!) to make a single narrative. In contrast to today's instant communication by e-mail, fax, phone or even mobile these letters had advantages as well as disadvantages. For instance I recall a written request from our Agents in Port Louis Mauritius to purchase a new tug desperately needed for lighterage work in that port. The case was well made out and costed so I forwarded it to London with strong recommendation that work on the new vessel should start without delay. Before a reply came we received another desperate request that delay was causing disruption in the port because of a build up of unmovable barges. So, confidently expecting acquiescence from London, permission was given to go ahead. Two weeks later the anticipated answer did come from London *but* in the negative. The new tug was emphatically *not* considered necessary by the managing Directors for the scatter cash agents in Port Louis. Dutifully we reported (by letter) to London that unfortunately permission had already been given due to our, as it proved wrongful, assumption that the Managing Directors would agree. After that the correspondence on the topic mercifully ceased! This was a perfect example of what was called in Calcutta a SABU. Nothing to do with the Elephant Boy but an acronym for 'Self-adjusting balls-up'.

Another potentially explosive mistake was when, somewhat dreamy, I was dictating late afternoon a letter to the Managing Directors in London. My stenographer was Sudhir-Babu, a dignified gentleman – excellent typist – who, particularly in the hot weather, had a wet handkerchief tucked into his shirt breast pocket, which encouraged an ever-broadening circle of damp. The approved ending to such letters to the great and good of HQ was 'we have the honour, gentlemen to be your most obedient servants . . .'. On this occasion I jokingly dictated '*Woppity wop wop wap, Love Jim*'. I was on the point of signing the submitted letter when I (happily) spotted '*Woppity* etc'. 'Sudhir,' I cried, 'what have you put here?' With solemn dignity Sudhir turned to his dictation pad and recited '*Woppity* etc'. 'That, my dear Sudhir,' I said, 'was Davis-Sahib's joke.' Gravely Sudhir went away to retype the offending paragraph.

All sorts of peculiarly Indian experiences made up the matrix of experience of living and working in Calcutta. Golf at the Royal Calcutta GC was a special feature. Playing in that great heat was something special as was the occasional experience of sharing a bunker with a deadly poisonous snake. The latter were always quickly dealt with by one's barefoot caddy! The caddies and 'Age Wallahs' were a study in themselves. The 'Age Wallah' was the additional caddy who went ahead particularly to observe and record the fall of shot (i.e. where ones ball had ended up . . . particularly valuable on a course peppered with lakes.) Many is the story of two 'burrah sahibs' playing blood matches against each other. One slices his shot straight into a lake ('tank' as they were known). The AW surreptitiously jumps in after the errant ball, picks it up with his toes and dumps in the middle of the fairway 'Gad, Featherstone', would exclaim the big man when he reached his ball 'I'm having a lucky day. Must have bounced off that pine over there!' Thus the caddies and AWs kept their Masters happy and produced, if that were considered appropriate, a halved match between the warring parties.

Once a year Mackinnons Calcutta, as Managing Agents, called in the Number Ones from the various Agencies ranging from the Persian (now Arabian) Gulf to Japan for a high level conference. Its effectiveness was hard to judge but the assembly of its extraordinarily eclectic group of gentlemen was fascinating. The level of debate was not very high. I recall the judgement of Kenneth Campbell (the Calcutta MD) after a debate on Maersk's invasion of the Far East/Bay of Bengal and Far East/PG routes. It was 'F_____ Maersk' which, though picturesque, was scarcely problem-solving.

Another triviality I remember from that conference was the description given by Tim Flanagan (later to be my Boss in Hong Kong when I moved there) of the No. 1 in Karachi: 'Smooth as a buttered turd'. Very descriptive!

During these conferences we juniors were moved out of our regular 'chummeries' and put up with friends. I moved in with a delightful group from Finlays in Harrington Mansions, a large block of flats on Chowringhee the main street of Calcutta alongside the huge Maidan. I especially remember it because during our sojourn there, there was a strike of schoolteachers. Strikers in India were generally non-violent or, more correctly, violent only against property rather than other people. Their favourite objects of attack were tramcars and street lights. I recall seeing a huge mob coming along Chowringhee and as they progressed each tramcar was set alight and each street lamp was extinguished. Since we had our company cars parked in our open driveway two of us – somewhat imprudently perhaps – went down to tell the raging mob not to touch our cars.

The response from the mob leadership was a touching 'Do not worry Sahib we have no quarrel with you and your garis (cars)'.

So with a polite exchange of words a very alarming mob bent on burning street cars and destroying street lights turned and continued their way.

Around that time Pandit Nehru came to make a speech on the Maidan. A crowd of more than a million was expected so a set of crush barriers and fencing had to be erected. This entailed the planting of upwards of 50,000 stout poles in the hard baked earth of the Maidan. The answer? Hire 50,000 admi (men) and all the poles were put in concurrently in a matter of minutes. A very Indian solution.

Apart from Golf – either very early morning or at weekends – there was little time for much recreation or proper holidays while I was in Calcutta. There was one weekend when a quartet of us, among them the more experienced (in India) 'Sandy' Marshall, drove North via Ranchi in a Vauxhall Velox to Netarhat, the site of a Dakh (hunting) Bungalow. What I remember most vividly was a collision with a bicycle rickshaw in Hazarebag.

No one was hurt, apart from a figure of eight wheel on the rickshaw, but we had to beat a hasty retreat as a frighteningly large hue and cry developed. Later the bearings on our nearside front wheel jammed. We squeaked our way into Ranchi where a little man ('Mistri', meaning mechanical expert!) himself created some new ball bearings over his own little brazier. The repair so expertly carried out cost every bit of £2 as I recall!

CHAPTER 5

The Far East

Towards the end of November I was advised that my next station was to be Kobe Japan. The prospect filled me with joy. Leaving Calcutta was – after all the dislike I had for the place during my time there – an occasion of mixed emotions. I left on the Bombay Mail from the frenetically crowded Howrah Station. It seemed always that some 1,000,000 people made it their permanent home and the general noise and confusion had to be seen to be believed. Nevertheless a large proportion of the Mackinnons staff plus my many other friends had set up a Bar-Buffet on the platform, so I pulled out of the station in a hazy, Scotch-filled state. I travelled 'first class' in the one such carriage in reasonable comfort. The 'air-conditioning' was created by blocks of ice in the roof with a big stir-about Punkah playing downwards. Until somewhere along the line – Hyderabad I think – I was alone in this huge carriage, but there a ruddy-faced Tea Planter joined. He was jolly enough company, his only demand to the bearer being that his chota peg of whisky be kept full during the whole period of the two-day journey. I should also mention that our circumstances were of superb luxury compared with our travelling companions in third class who filled each compartment with 30-odd people who slept on, under and above (in the luggage racks) the seats. Even they were in excellent comfort compared with scores of others clinging to the outside and on the roof of each carriage (except of course the first class one!).

I had a couple of days in Bombay, which seemed like Scarborough when compared with poor old Calcutta, before boarding *Corfu* for the Far East. This voyage took us to Colombo, Penang and Singapore thence to Hong Kong. It was an enjoyable trip. Playing with Bill Campbell, subsequently Managing Director of BI, we won the ship's bridge tournament before discovering that we were playing entirely different bidding conventions from one another. It certainly explained some very curious bidding which must have confused our succession of opponents much more than it did ourselves.

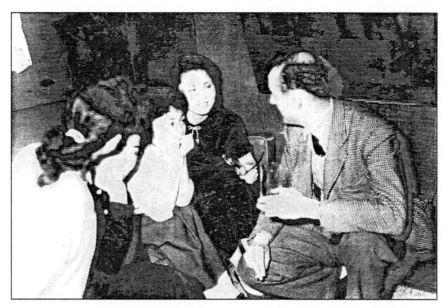

A sad sayonara from the very sweet girls of our Kobe Office before I sailed off in 'Shillong' (See page 51)

The Corfu, *between Singapore and Hong Kong*

Like every other first-time visitor Hong Kong completely beguiled me, so beautiful a harbour with such breathtaking vitality. After a few days there I embarked in China Navigation's *Anking* for Yokohama. I was somewhat alarmingly forewarned that a fellow passenger was to be 'Ma' Barrow, Mother of my Boss-to-be in Kobe. She had a fearsome reputation and Bobbie Barrow was reputedly totally under her command and lived a protracted bachelor existence ... in Japan of all places! The reality of 'Ma' B proved to be, so far as I personally was concerned, totally different from her reputation. Indeed she was tough but was kindness itself to anyone she liked. I had no cause to be in awe of her and we got on swimmingly from day one.

It was curious to arrive in Japan just a few days before Christmas. The country seemed very strange and I knew nobody. For a day or two I stayed with Duncan and Rita Macfarlane at their very nice company house on the Bluff in Yokohama. Duncan was a white haired (prematurely because he could not have been more than late forties at the time) scholarly man who spoke and wrote perfect Japanese. Never have I met a more gentle and considerate person.

His natural career should have been as an academic far from the world of commerce but his charm and manners made him a great favourite of the Japanese with considerable commercial benefit to the P&O Group. Incidentally he undertook the task of translating and editing the Autobiography of Mr Ariyoshi (the legendary post-war President of NYK (Nippon Yusen Kaisha) who restored that great company to its pre-eminent position in Japanese Shipping).

It was all very strange as I sat alone in front of a log fire attended by kimono-clad maids on Christmas Eve. My only other companion was 'Badger', a large distinctly unfriendly chow-type dog who eyed me with deep suspicion. I felt very sorry for myself as I thought of family, friends and (conspicuously) girl friends.

Shortly after Christmas I left Yokohama to take up residence in Kobe. It was a long train ride, being years before the Shinkansen (the 'Bullet' train) was introduced on its specially built high speed track. The southern (Kansai) part of Honshu Island was, particularly in the fifties, very different from the North (Kanto). Kobe being at the entrance of the Inland Sea and in the Shadow of Mount Rokko is beautifully situated and in those days was linked to the huge city of Osaka by the Hanshin Kokado, a large pot-holed highway.

Having no pre-arranged accommodation I spent the first two weeks at the house of my boss in Kobe, Bobbie Barrow, and my newly acquired friend 'Ma' Barrow. This generous arrangement did however have great disadvantages since the Barrows favoured a Virginia Water style of existence with a series of ex-patriot dinner parties, bridge parties and the rest. The guests were the other company heads (Dunlop, ICI, Shell etc) plus the large population of Lloyds Register Surveyors. all very nice people but giving me little chance to increase my knowledge of Japan. Furthermore their house was situated some miles outside Kobe along the coast in an area adjacent to the beautiful Shioya Country Club.

But everything changed when a flat was found and I moved in, accompanied by a marvellous middle-aged 'Cook-San' (really House-keeper and Factotum) who catered for my every need. Early on I displayed my enjoyment of strawberries and cream – strawberries being available year-long in Japan -and as a result my dear Cook-San served them every day for the rest of my time in the country!

The address: Sassoon Apartments
        Yamamoto-dori
        Ni-Chome
        Kobe
Plus the phone number – 2-8327 – is indelibly printed in my mind.

There was a very sporty band of bachelors in Kobe who quickly became my out-of-school friends plus, it must be said, a wonderfully eclectic number of ex-patriot families. My neighbours were the delightful Dick English, the General Manager of Dunlop Japan and his wife Betty.

Things developed rapidly. I was certainly busy enough, being responsible for all the P&O ships plus, significantly, the Eastern & Australian Line, which operated a freight liner service between Australia and the Far East. There were a range of duties to perform.

At that time also troop ships were regularly coming to Kure – adjacent to Hiroshima – maintaining the UK's considerable 'occupy-ing' presence in Japan, but which was dominated by the US. There were some fine old ships continuing their wartime role such as *Asturias* of Royal Mail, plus post-war troopers such as *Nevasa*, *Dunera* and *Devonshire*. I gained experience of Southern Japan by taking the train regularly to Hiroshima to service those ships. My knowledge of the Japanese language though fast improving was rudimentary or worse in the early months, which meant that communication with the locals like train ticket inspectors was perilously hard. In 1953 English was very little spoken in the country.

Another monthly journey was across to Yokkaichi adjacent to Nagoya which was the first port of call, being the site of the clothing industry, for the E & A Ships coming up from Sydney with their consignments of wool. We had great evenings in Yokkaichi in the vast 'Swing Swing Star' Ballroom : a bachelor's paradise. As one left the ballroom the girls discreetly whispered their number and name; I still remember 422, Sadako-san!

E & A itself was a splendidly run company with unrivalled Australian management. The ships' complement consisted of Australian Officers and Chinese Deck and Engine-room crews. The ships were spotless. Everything – derricks, windlass, ventilators – shone with daily washed gloss paint, and this despite the fact that the ships were without exception wartime-built second-hand vessels. *Nellore* and *Eastern* were large Empire Class while *Nankin* was an American constructed Victory ship. The latter was a superbly efficient cargo carrying vehicle (high reinforced between decks, strong slab hatches etc) but with no aesthetic beauty and distinctly Spartan accommodation. The day came however when instead of its usual 'Second hand Rose' treatment E & A took delivery of its first custom built ship *Arafura*. She arrived at Yokkaichi gleaming with her Barclay Curle applied paintwork. A very large Australian, 'Aub' Johnston, was Chief Officer. 'Well, how do you like your new baby? 'I asked Aub when I boarded in Yokkaichi. 'She's a beaut, Jim,' said Aub. 'Built for the Trade . . . unfortunately not this one!'

He was, alas, correct. We needed uncluttered open decks for the carriage of livestock in stalls: there somehow seemed to be obstructions (ventilators or whatever) scattered randomly all over the deck. We needed maximum lock-up and refrigerated space, the former vital for the carriage of ammunition: there was insufficient of both. *Arafura* represented the very worst failing of shipowners of the time who saw their job as producing and running ships – that delightful yet dangerous word '*Skibsreder*', as the Scandinavians called themselves – rather than having to soil their hands and minds with the task of filling the ships and having a profound understanding of the market and the customers that their ships were serving. That part of the activity was blithely left to shipbrokers and freight brokers, a lesser breed.

I must confess that the production of *Arafura* was a classic example
of the lack of commercial spirit that existed in many areas of my
beloved P&O. 'One must make clear to these shippers that it is a real
privilege for them to have their cargoes carried in P&O ships,' joked
Andrew (later Sir Andrew) Crichton to me when I was working with
him in the sixties back in Head Office.

I instituted a regular – two days a week – trek to Osaka to meet
the major trading houses of the Kansai. Mitsui Bussan, Daiichi Busan,
Tatsuta Kyogyo, C. Itoh and the rest. This was before all those
business houses moved their Head Offices to the Kanto-Tokyo and
Yokohama-in the sixties . . . a thoroughly retrograde step in my view.

The Shioya Country Club was beautifully situated looking over
Awaji Island and the Inland Sea, and had a vigorous social existence.
I played a lot of tennis there and was also persuaded to take the lead
in one of their annual amateur dramatic productions. The Japanese
people were then – as now – charming and courteous, the girls and
women having a self-effacing sweetness which was utterly beguiling.
So few years after the horrors of the Pacific war and its bloody
conclusion at Hiroshima and Nagasaki, it was very hard to get one's
mind round the fact that it was these same people who had
committed some of the most heinous and callous war crimes ever
known.

A good acquaintance was the Barman at the High Ball Bar, which
I frequently used as a watering-hole after seeing off my midnight
sailings. He had been trained as a Kame Kazi pilot, one of those who
would take off from a carrier with fuel enough only to reach their
target and with the cockpit hood screwed down to discourage any
unlikely change of heart, to crash their plane into an enemy ship.
They had been trained ('brain washed'?) to positively look forward
to this final act of loyalty to their Emperor and Dai Nippon. The final
weeks prior to their sortie was dedicated to sensual earthly pleasures
of wine and women (lots). He had been spared at the last minute by
the war's unexpectedly early conclusion speeded by the atomic bomb
attacks. A more normal individual it would be hard to find and he
was devoid of any bitterness over the whole affair.

One who came into my life in 1954 and became one of my most
cherished friends was John Moore. He joined McKinnons Japan and
worked under my initial tutorship in the spring of that year. He was
of mixed antecedence and really had two names. One was Ogle John

de Heez Moore – a distant Scion of the Earls of Drogheda – the other was simply Hiroshi Wakamatsu. In 1941 he had been at Bedford School, and was a public school accented, though Japanese looking, product of such an upbringing.

Before Pearl Harbour was attacked on 7 December 1941 he together with other Japanese working in the UK were shipped back to Japan. John was a subject of great distrust but was rapidly recruited into the Imperial Japanese Army. His knowledge of the Japanese language was less than perfect and meant that he could given only a low-security posting. The front line in Manchuria seemed admirably to meet this requirement, and there he was subject to appalling privation to say nothing of consistent antagonism and bullying from Officers, non coms and fellow soldiers. Even today I find it hard to envisage that life meted out to a young person whose previous life had hitherto been so totally different in every respect. A mild kit offence was punished by standing all night outside in the frozen Manchurian winter with a bucket of water in each hand.

When he joined the company however he had somehow preserved a wonderful balance and sense of humour. He rapidly became my friend and my mentor in all things Japanese. The 'real' Japanese life as opposed to the 'Geijin' (foreigners') style was opened for me by John and we had some marvellous experiences together in for instance the Minami-district of Osaka. The Japanese bars there were quite something.

John Moore and I became great friends I taught him about ships and shipping while he taught me about Japan and life in general. He for instance warned me that Society was likely to treat me as a performing seal (i.e. without delving further would tend to see only my superficial personality as a good dinner guest, a good speechifier etc). He was pretty accurate.

One amusing, if humbling experience I had – without John this time – was in the famed hot spring resort of Yunoyama near Nagoya. I went there with our Agent and Stevedore. An early requirement was to don a 'yukata' (robe) and proceed down the street to a specially beautiful o-furo (hot bath). Two other Japanese from the same inn walked down there with us. My Yukata was absurdly small, hardly reaching my knees, yet – amusing as it looked – I was very surprised to find the whole street lined on both sides by giggling teenage girls. I had no idea that I was so engaging a sight. However we four proceeded to our hot bath and chatted somewhat haltingly immersed up to our necks.

Back in the hotel I remarked on the strange slightly unnerving behaviour of all those pretty little Japanese girls. My host laughed. 'I am very sorry to disappoint you. Davis-San, but it was not you that those young ladies were admiring. One of those other gentlemen was Hasengawa Kasuo-San and it was him that they longed to see'. Apparently Hasengawa was at that time *the* most popular stage and film actor in Japan, a sort of combination of Laurence Olivier, Gregory Peck and Clark Gable.

And so my time in Japan passed. Undoubtedly it was one of the happiest periods in my life professionally and socially. There were all kinds of minor incidents that increased my affection for Japan and its people, e.g. eating Sukiyaki with the girls of the Takarazuka Girls Opera (a rare privilege which was described in the novel *Sayonara*) . . . I won a bet that I could not achieve this enviable experience, so protected were those beautiful girls! There were visits to o-furos (hot spring resorts), playing at Hirono Golf course, then the most prestigious in Japan, the geisha parties given by for instance the Directors of Kawasaki Dockyard upon completion of a successful Ship's Special Survey. A memorable feature of the latter was the gentle passing out one by one of one's hosts. The Japanese tolerance level of sake is markedly below that of foreigners. Thus I frequently found myself with an '*embarras de richesse*' entertaining as many as six beautiful geishas after all the hosts had gone deeply asleep.

The sporting side of life was also vigorous. The KR&AC (Kobe Regatta and Athletics Club) had regular matches of tennis, rugby, hockey and soccer against all the local universities (Waseda, Keio etc) and the season ended with matches against Yokohama C&AC in all the sports.

Each weekend therefore on top of tennis I regularly played soccer and hockey following on each other the same afternoon with rugger on the other day. Youth is a wonderful thing indeed! How I managed it amid all my other activities, particularly the evening ones, I really don't know.

There were also 'healthy' picnics on the island of Awaji, so described by Bridget Jacques, one of the Kobe wives, designed as a contrast or antidote to the lives we bachelors were living day-by-day in Kobe.

Above all was the sheer enjoyment of working with the ever cheerful and enthusiastic staff of our Kobe office. Everyone was visibly thrilled each time we exceeded our monthly earnings on our various (freight) sailings.

Leaving Japan was a terrible wrench. The Japanese are sentimental folk and came in flocks to see me off on our (P&O's) cargo ship *Shillong*. Apart from my many English friends there were representatives from all our shippers, the dockyards, Kobe Ship Repair plus of course our entire office staff, supported by the Kobe Town Band. My cook-san and my very favourite tiny little office junior Mutsuko Tateiwa were in floods of tears and I nearly succumbed myself. I subsequently had a most touching letter from Mr Endoh of Mitsui-Bussan which is in appendix A. As *Shillong* pulled away from the Wharf thousands of streamers broke; it was like the departure of a huge passenger ship. There is something heart rending at seeing the last streamer break, representing the last tangible link severed. I had a whisky and went up to the bridge to see Kobe fade into the distance, particularly the huge neon sign of 'Kawasaki Dockyard' mounted on their transverse crane. The captain, Eric Spurling, remarked later in the voyage that never before had anyone, even a putative member of management, drunk a whisky on his bridge, but such was the emotion of that sailing from Kobe he felt obliged not to intervene.

It is hard – even at this distance of years – to describe just how profound an affect my years in Japan had on me.

I encountered nothing but courtesy and friendship from the Japanese people. They were recovering from an ultimately devastating defeat in World War 2, which they had fought with a fanaticism previously unknown to the West. Having lost however they simply bowed before their 'conquerors' and were genuinely surprised at the generally compassionate treatment they received. Also they set about rebuilding their shattered economy with total enthusiasm. For instance DK Ludwig had acquired the, now IHI Shipyard adjacent to Kure/Hiroshima and was building ships of unprecedented size at unprecedented speed. I recall my own astonishment at seeing a line of *55,000* dwt Bulk Carriers. This, remember, was back in 1954.

I have not revisited Kobe for a few years. I often wonder how many of my favourite little restaurants, bars, geisha houses etc not to mention my old friends or their offspring may have been destroyed in that dreadful earthquake of 1995.

It was indeed a heavy hearted voyage as we made our way through the Inland Sea and on through the Shimonoseki Strait toward Shanghai. I particularly recall two of the other passengers.

One, on a round voyage from London, was a peppery rather small man called Mr Scharnhorst. He was making a voyage of a lifetime having devoted his working life to the manufacture of sausage casings (he was most adamant about this description . . . 'skins' simply was not correct).

I remember him particularly because of his indignation against the swarms of Red Guards who came aboard the ship as we entered the Yangtse River in Shanghai. These cold-eyed young men carrying definitely loaded, automatic weapons stopped one at every juncture on the ship once they had done their initial task of sealing the Radar, the Wireless Room and even the compass! Mr Scharnhorst was so incensed by these frightening Maoist fighters that he said to me in their hearing (fortunately I don't believe they understood) that he was seriously considering writing to his MP which, said he, would bring those guards to heel. This at a time when Maoist frenzy was at white heat and when any dissenter ('Capitalist Railroader') whether Chinese or foreign could be arrested and disappear without trial struck me as remarkably incongruous! Shanghai at the time was indeed frightening. The other was an Irish Girl who had been working in Tokyo but was on her way to marrying a Swede working in China for Ekman Foreign Agencies. She was most understanding of my sadness at leaving Japan and counselled me not to think that I had so early in life found my Shangri-la.

The guards appointed to *Shillong* took most of the thoroughly bewildered Indian crew for a Chinese banquet while the Europeans, especially me, as an identifiable Capitalist Shipowner exploiter were given hostile looks.

I was however taken ashore by our 'Agent', actually *four* serious-faced Chinese who presumably were charged with the task of watching not only me but each other. I recall the guard at the bottom of the gangway taking my Passport and examining it with great thoroughness until he reached the page with my picture on it when he realized he had been reading it upside down. He looked up sharply to see whether I was smirking at his discomfiture. I certainly wasn't.

It was a grim 'sightseeing' tour that the 'Agents' gave me. Maotse Tung happened to be in town and the security surrounding the Great

Helmsman was extreme. I actually saw him through a huge crowd of his admiring countrymen.

We drove through the old and hugely impressive former Shanghai Horse Racetrack. No longer were horses to be seen but instead the grandstand had become the People's Library and the course the people's Parade Ground and Vista. Books abounded on the stalls in the streets but the choice of reading seemed confined to little red books entitled 'The Thoughts of Chairman Mao'. Naturally I bought an English edition and, even allowing for unsympathetic translation, I have never encountered such tautological rubbish/garbage!

China had many more years of suffering ahead as Mao became more and more erratic. The 'Great Leap Forward', the 'Cultural Revolution', were yet to come and the people phlegmatically endured them. I have visited China very many times since, but this first occasion left me with an enduring impression of the fear and the sheer drabness which were the main features of life under such an oppressive system.

And so on to Hong Kong and on this portion of the voyage there was an exciting little incident when our main generator packed up. Being a steam turbine Vessel, *Shillong* quickly lost power and stopped. We anchored. Just after the anchor had gone a very large junk fleet hove into view creating some anxiety as piracy was especially active in that area in 1956. In an agonizingly long time a repair was made and the last remaining steam power was used to start up the generator. If this had failed we would have been put into the supremely embarrassing, not to say perilous position of being unable to raise anchor. Captain Spurling gently asked me, 'Shall we go for it?' We did and it worked, not that there was much alternative!

Hong Kong was a huge contrast to Japan. It was, then as later, a bustling port and an astonishingly successful combination of Chinese, Indian and other Oriental diligence and inventiveness and British Colonial Style governance. It was not yet the financial centre that it became in the seventies and eighties. It was in fact the entrepôt Port for the millions of tons of Chinese products that arrived daily from the mainland predominantly in Junks. One of Hong Kong's prime industries seemed to be the production of forged Certificates of Origin to overcome the US embargo on PRC products.

Hong Kong society was defined by a British pecking order of the Governor and his staff (Financial Secretary, Colonial secretary etc) the armed forces and the 'significant' major companies (Butterfield & Swire, Jardines, J.D. Hutchinson, P&O /BI/ represented by Mackinnon Mackenzie) and so on.

With comparatively few exceptions there was little social intercourse with the indigenous Hong Kongese. The great entrepreneurs like Li Ka Shing, Y K Pao, Wah Kwong, the Chao family and the Tungs were vigorously on the move but were far from the mammoth figures they rapidly became. The population was just over 2 million in contrast to today's 7 ½ million.

It was already a consumer's paradise but not yet the tourist destination it soon became. Indeed there were only three 'good' hotels: the Peninsula, the Gloucester and the Repulse Bay. The resident major regiment with its 1,000 odd members to face up to the several million Red army troops ranged on the border facing the New Territories was the 7th Hussars. We simple commercial folk thought of their officer corps qualities as being (1) A profound sense of self importance (2) a thinly disguised contempt for those 'in trade' and (3) the ownership of very large feet which had to be accommodated and passed through very narrow trousers.

Though Hong Kong was adored by many 'ex-Pats' I found it a totally less interesting place in which to live and work in contrast to my beloved Kansai district of Japan. The harsh character of the Hong Kong Chinese, characterized by the noisy Cantonese language, made a stark contrast with the Japanese, especially the latters' gently mannered and soft-spoken women folk.

I think it was the day after I arrived that Alan Cook, an exact Alan Whicker look-alike, whom I was relieving, left for the UK, so the 'handover' was somewhat brief! I took up the desk of BI (some 20 ships a month North and Southbound) and the Knutsen Line.

I lived in a flat on top the P&O building (then one of Hong Kong's tallest at seven storeys) so my journey to the office was short indeed, which was just as well in that my days usually started around 6.30 a.m. going out in the launch to welcome the incoming ships in Lyemun Bay and frequently ended well after midnight having seen off departing ships and signed literally hundreds sometimes thousands, of Bills of Lading that Chinese Shippers would be clamouring to pick up early the following morning.

Thus it was a busy life but not without many pleasures. I managed to fit in a certain amount of golf at Fanling and Shek-O. Launch picnics, which became all the rage in the sixties, did not yet figure. A visit to Macau by overnight steamer provided a nice break from frenzied Hong Kong. My Cambridge friend, Ronnie Kidd, who had been British consul in Kobe, had been translated to be Temporary Consul General in Macau, and it was interesting to spend a few days in the then completely 'Old Colonial' lifestyle there: it was a manifestation of a foreign office apparent rule that a language expert (Ronnie was a trained Japanese speaker) should be transferred to Cantonese/ Portuguese speaking Macau. We believed similarly that the appointments were made alphabetically (i.e. China would be followed by Colombia, Honduras by Hungary, Poland by Portugal etc!)

My colleagues in Hong Kong were assuredly an amusing lot. Tim Flanagan, the Managing Director was witty and amusing. He had passed many years in Shanghai during the 'good' days, while George Tagg the No.2 had similarly been for years in Singapore and Malaya. Both were unbelievably idle yet equally agreeable and left one alone to do one's job with no interference whatsoever.

Gerry Salmon my colleague on the other Agency Desk was a very able operator though rather unkindly contemptuous of our two seniors – but he was a splendid companion and brilliant pianist, mostly self-taught. His signature tune was Norman Wisdom's 'Don't laugh at me 'cos I'm a fool!' Long after my time Gerry himself became the No. 1 of Mackinnons Hong Kong and a member of the 'Legco', the advisory body under the Governor (healthily unelected in those splendid times), which ruled the colony of Hong Kong. For this he was awarded the OBE.

Fred, the P&O Shore Bo'sun, who ran our beautiful launches which served the ships, was the most comic undiscovered artful dodger on our payroll. He also had the 'job' of awarding passes to approved traders who wished to ply their wares on the ships. This was something capable of mind-bending graft and Fred conducted the operation to his great personal satisfaction. Despite this he was an attractive character with an appealing whole-hearted love of life. Upon retirement from P&O he spent a number of years as 'Transport Manager' of the newly constructed Mandarin Hotel (incidentally still water in my time) where he controlled the hotel's fleet of Rolls Royces and Mercedes. Right up his street.

I took 'local leave' over the Christmas period 1956/7 to re-visit Japan. I sailed up in *Sangola* a BI passenger/cargo ship on the Bay of

Bengal/Japan run. Her magnificently bearded Captain 'Baldy' Davies from Barry, South Wales I had known well over the years and it was a fun trip. If I dared a siesta I was woken by 'Baldy's' servant with the injunction to 'Get out of your scratcher and play ping-pong with the Captain'. A feature of the voyage was when we found ourselves in the middle, literally, of the US 6th Fleet which in those days was obdurately circling Formosa/Taiwan to create an effective barrier between the 'new' China and the mainland.

It was a very happy Christmas and New Year in Japan and I renewed friendships with my old friends male and female, ex-patriots and Japanese. Jimmy Brown who had taken over from Bobbie Barrow as Director in Kobe gave a splendid dinner in my honour at the company's Shukugawa House where, to my amusement, my place-card at the table had the single name: 'Lt Pinkerton'.

Visiting the countryside and various o-furos (hot springs) was delightful, marred only by one drive when I experienced two punctures within minutes!

Back in Hong Kong there was the usual activity. One's rapport with the Ships' Captains was immensely rewarding and two truthful anecdotes give the picture.

Harry ('China Blue Eyes') Blake was Captain of *Olinda*, a 10-knot BI Ocean Greyhound. His arrival signal in which was given ETA, gangs required, etc etc never ended without the words 'Onion Soup 7.45 at Jimmy's Kitchen,' the indication that whatever was happening elsewhere he wanted dinner with me at his favourite HK restaurant. Son of a country vicar he had a tremendous sense of humour and matchless manners and charm. On one voyage he had a supremely incompetent Chief Officer who had spent long years in the troopships. Returning to less glamorous cargo ships this officer maintained his RN style bearing, the while making a total mess of his cargo stowage. He bafflingly succeeded in over-stowing cargo and generally getting everything wrong – and this ultimately reflected on his Captain in the eyes of 'Management'. However Harry remained totally calm and smilingly confided to me 'Can't be angry with him, Jim, he's so frightfully polite'.

'Jimmy' Wild, a P&O Captain who subsequently became Com-modore of the Fleet (together with a CBE) was my absolute favourite. As an earlier Captain of *Shillong* he was ever conscious of profitability in terms both of cost control and, even more maximizing earnings. On one occasion when I was 'controlling' the homeward loading from Hong Kong I had occasion to radio him enquiring whether he could accept cargo from Trincomalee when his ship had already been totally filled apart from one tween deck and hatch square.

The radios went roughly thus:

JGD: Know how full you are but any chance your accepting x tons of tea from Trinco?

Jimmy W: Having, as you well know, taken on oranges from Indonesia I only have space in that same hatch and oranges taint tea if in the same hatch.

JGD: Appreciate that. Shall I reject Trinco?

Jimmy W: Can you check London Tea Market?

JGD: Yes. There is a technical shortage and market rising fast.

Jimmy W: Accept Tea. On a rising Market oranges don't taint.

This is only one example of Jimmy's tangential thinking. He adored horse-racing, reading, national as well as company politics ('It's easy for me Jim. I just have to keep my nose clean and I shall end up at the top. You, on the other hand, have to compete with all the winds and forces of a corporate life. I wonder if you are a sufficient S__t to win!'). More of him later, but he was a delight to work with.

Another well remembered friend was Wong Chi Po the Compradore for Mackinnons/P&O Group. The Compradore's function was to act as an intermediary/guarantor for the myriad of Chinese Shippers, (for an interesting 'cut') and to act as supplier of various husbandry items. He was typically shrewd in business, was very boyish in his enthusiasms and quintessentially Chinese in his attitude to life and family. We became fast friends. If he joined me and others on many a night out Chi Po (who did not carry his drink too well) was in the habit of going to a jewellers, of whom he was the landlord, and taking home a handful of diamond bracelets, watches and rings as a peace offering to Julie, his placid, beautiful if long suffering wife. It was usually I who delivered him home to his spectacularly splendid house on the mid-levels of the Peak. The savage Alsatian guard dogs were secured and in we went where he laid out the diamonds, watches etc on his bar counter saying 'Julie, my love, my darling – for you!' Julie gathered them up with a gentle smile and delivered them next day back to the disappointed shop-owner.

I should also mention the splendid Norwegian Captains of the Knutsen ships *Kristin Bakke* (Emil Olsen) and *Ellen Bakke* (John

Fagerland – the latter a recipient of the OBE for making the most tanker crossings of the Atlantic during World War 2). Their ships were beautifully run and very modern. Another of them *Elisabeth Bakke* obtained a special fame. She was sailing – the only ship southbound that evening – to Singapore when news reached the Vegetable Shippers in Hong Kong that Singapore had suddenly reached a crisis shortage in the Vegetable Market. Dozen upon dozen of junks arrived alongside *Elisabeth* with the Shippers beseeching that their cargo be taken despite her departure time having been reached. I discussed this with the Captain and Chief Officer, who agreed to wait (no doubt, I suspected though never knew (!) – there having passed certain inducements). At last when she sailed her decks were piled high with the deck cargo of cabbages which nearly obscured the view forward from the Bridge. On arrival at Singapore the Market was at an unprecedented high and the Hong Kong Shippers made an equally unprecedented killing. For this service *Elisabeth* became Hong Kong's favourite ship, a 'lucky' ship, and was awarded a 150-foot 'Joss flag' to be worn whenever in Hong Kong. The practical benefit of this was that *Elisabeth* made record earnings on every visit. Even when more modern, faster transit, opposition vessels were competing on the berth *Elisabeth* had scores of junks alongside while the other ships had a miserable few. This was a beautiful example of the Chinese psyche.

What do I best remember about my days in Hong Kong? Inevitably the extraordinary dynamic activity and sheer optimism of the place was pretty intoxicating. It was a shoppers' paradise, particularly in terms of luxury goods, hand made shoes and bespoke tailored suits.

My Amah, Ah Kwan, who looked after me, assisted by a younger girl, Ah Lin, provided amazing service. Ah Kwan was an able cook and totally unflappable would produce an excellent meal for six (whom I in jolly mood had invited with 20 minutes notice . . . a pretty thoughtless act) in no time at all. She was an ardent Buddhist and a leader of all the local amahs and I would frequently find her of an evening surrounded by her friends conducting her devoted 'Jin Jin Josh' sessions. She served me in a charming motherly way.

Then there were the office staff who were tremendous workers and thoroughly efficient even when for instance my section Chief Clerk Mr Hui was occasionally a trifle disoriented from the previous nights mah-jong and opium.

I shall never forget also an unusual incident in Taikoo Dockyard. *Aronda*, a passenger cargo ship on the then West Pakistan (Karachi)/ East Pakistan (Chittagong) service via Colombo came up to Hong Kong for a routine General Survey. She entered the Taikoo Graving Dock without incident but then an enthusiastic Chinese fitter removed the Port Main Injection when the dock was still more than half full. The consequence was a catastrophic flooding of the engine room and the ship gently heeled over to 45° and came to rest with her superstructure resting against the dockside. Informed of this I went down to the dockyard meanwhile (it was Saturday) informing George Tagg who, with Tim Flanagan on leave in the UK, was the Director in charge of Hong Kong at the time. George was at the golf course and, when reached, said to me 'Jim old boy I think it best if you handled it' and hung up. Actually it was an excellent experience and I had to think quickly of the mass of people who needed to be told, and mobilized. A day or so later the dreaded duo of Donald Lattin (Chief Marine Supt BI) and George Cruickshank (Chief Engineer Supt BI) arrived from Calcutta who, from the time I picked them up at Kai Tak airport until *Aronda* was safely salved and repaired, provided me with endless amusement coupled with very late nights. The delivery of a case of his favourite Scotch to his room in the Gloucester Hotel was George's first request.

The Hong Kong of today is totally different. 'Fragrant Harbour', the singular entrepot port for the trade of China became, from the sixties onwards, a financial centre and steadily the World's largest container port handling now nearly 20 million Teus per annum. What was water in my time is now land (even where the now venerable Mandarin Hotel stands was water then).

There was no harbour tunnel and all cross harbour travel was by Star Ferry or the Vehicular Yaumati Ferries.

Such shipping dynasties as World Wide (Y.K. Pao), Wah Kwong (T.Y. Chao) and C.Y. Tung were very much in their infancy, buying their first ships. The 'Hongs', Butterfield & Swire, Jardine Matheson, J.D. Hutchinson plus the Mardens and of course P&O and BI, (Mackinnon Mackenzie) dominated the Commercial scene.

The population was less than a third of that today.

It was a different World.

The journey home was in *Chusan* under Captain 'Jackie' Last the Commodore, a tiny man with a deep voice and an unmatched reputation as a seaman and shiphandler. He was also a fanatical deck-tennis player. Another fascinating aspect of Capt. Last's make-up was that he was not in the least interested in ships qua ships. A seaman supreme, he feigned – and I do not think he was simulating – not to be able to recognize any other ship.

The Passenger List was an extremely eclectic collection, a large number of whom joined in Singapore and Penang, having been 'Malayanized'. They were ex-patriot, usually British Administrators Judges etc whose jobs had been subsumed by local Malay, Singaporeans and Chinese. Add to these some splendid retiring rubber planters and everyone was in a very happy end-of-term frame of mind. Another more exotic party joined in Colombo, being the production team and some of the cast of Bridge on the River Kwai which had been filmed in Ceylon/Sri Lanka. Bill Holden himself came on board to see off the 'Kwai' team.

Another fellow passenger was Pat R.,[1] the son of a former Managing Director of P&O who was retiring as 'No. 1' of Penang. The most desperately stupid though 'fun' man Pat revealed a previously unknown talent on that voyage. He lit a cigarette before diving into the ship's pool then swam a length underwater and popped up at the other end with the cigarette (which by some contortion of the lips he had reversed inside his mouth) still alight! A great party piece.

Yet another was Tony, a charming vague character who had developed the unusual habit of proposing marriage to every young lady of whom he had become fond. Without exception they all accepted, leading to all manner of subsequent problems when reality re-emerged. His 'score' was already some 7 when a whole team of famous tennis players came to Calcutta. After a few days Tony had become engaged to 'Gorgeous Gussie Moran' – she of the frilly knickers who had recently delighted Wimbledon. It lasted just a few days after which he was posted by an infuriated No 1 to the

---

[1]This seems a somewhat dismissive description of Pat – the truth is, though, that he was representative of a company ethos that 'protected' the scions of P&O 'greats' and gave them where at all possible, comfortable postings. Pat was one such. He was most agreeable but not over-endowed with brains and certainly not with any commercial abilities. Gerry Salmon (see Hong Kong above) served under him in Penang and one day after a major tiffin, Pat came back excitedly into the office to say he had booked X thousand tons for Rajula next day for Madras. In fact Rajula was sailing in the opposite direction. Gerry had to reprimand his boss and repeat for the umpteenth time that in no circumstances should Pat undertake any business work!

'punishment post' of Chittagong, presumable to test what he could find there. On reflection I wonder why nothing happened on *Chusan*, though by then I think he was already married, for the first and last time.

Everyone got on, which was as well because the voyage was an exceptionally long one due to the closure of the Suez Canal. We sailed down to Durban and Capetown before coming North alongside the huge Continent of Africa, thence to Las Palmas – a 'cheap' oil bunkering port – and home, to Tilbury.

CHAPTER 6

Back home 1957

I HAD GIVEN TO MY beloved P&O four-plus years of my life away from home, family and friends – an experience which though fruitful in so many ways was a most definite sacrifice. The experience 'bound one with hoops of steel' to the company which had been at once employer, protector, landlord and friend for those long years. (Pay was another matter and was scarcely generous, though with prudence I had at least broken even over the period.) Those who have not shared this experience – such as those who run P&O today, including Jeffrey Sterling and his team – can never understand the bond that was created by 'living' the company in this way.

Homecoming had certain problems. I had been away for a long time and had undergone a lot of very different experiences. At the same time things had moved on back in the UK. Thus one felt somewhat isolated and 'different'. Obviously my mother and father particularly (he now being retired and not especially happy with that fact) were greatly looking forward to my return and my settling back into the old routine. Roy, now qualified and working phenomenal hours as a houseman at the Middlesex Hospital and St Thomas's was his old self, but silently rather envied the broader world that I had been experiencing. Going home to Dovercourt struck me as being thoroughly restrictive and was something that I did not handle very well. In retrospect I am sure that I hurt my parents by wanting to get away to stay with friends from the East with whom I felt more at ease. However the unease fairly quickly passed and I ultimately enjoyed the few months' leave I was given before reporting back to P&O in October 1957. There was a morale-sapping period during which Walter Kerr and I were given a series of quasi-auditing jobs reporting on the activities of various internal departments (e.g. the quite extraordinary rivalry between the Export and Import Freight Departments whose Managers and staff of each seemed to expend great effort in threatening the success and plans of the other Department). Such an audit by a Student Prince was not calculated to engender much affection from those being reported on! We also did some interesting research into such matters as the activities and aspirations of various Unions, particularly the TGWU and the NUS. It seemed nevertheless rather an aimless period designed to keep us busy while it was decided what to do with two embryo Management candidates. Finally the decision was made. Walter Kerr, now married, was to go back out to Bombay for a further 18 months, while I was to join Malcolm Millar, the Director in charge of the Passenger side, as his PA/Deputy.

I was very lucky. Malcolm was a delightful massive man and he gave me immediate access to his entire job including all correspondence, minutes of meetings etc etc. He was amusing to work with and consistently friendly. We had to overview every aspect of the passenger ship operations, scheduling, rate structures, on-line services, advertising, cruising etc, and I rapidly knew I had much to learn.

There was also the need for cooperation and liaison with the Orient Company which up until then was separately managed.

A major feature of the time was the decision to build two 'super' passenger ships for the Australian Route, one to be operated by P&O, the other by Orient. Up to this decision the design of passenger ships had been osmotic. There was little if any new thinking, and successive ships were an extension of the old, just larger and faster but of essentially the same lay out. By contrast the two new 40,000-plus newbuilds were to be innovative. One, P&O's *Canberra*, was distinctly so. With turbo-electric engines aft and a whole new general arrangement she was to be quite distinctive. Her designer was a young enthusiast John West and the Management bravely supported him despite the misgivings and mutterings of the in-house Naval Architects. John West was given junior manager status, which proved reasonably protective. The contract was given to Harland & Wolff who had constructed the beautiful if overweight *Iberia*.

Orient decided on a much more conventional layout, employing their in-house NA Team.

Oriana, built at Vickers Armstrong's, Barrow, proved to be a very effective, fast ship, even though possessing a quite extraordinarily ugly profile with a flowerpot-shaped funnel and another mini flowerpot further aft containing auxiliary exhausts and air-conditioning equipment.

I was given the extra job of overlooking the general – non-technical – construction of *Canberra* and of planning the introduction of the ship. Sir Hugh Casson was given responsibility for designing many of the Public Rooms of the ship, and being a kind of 'buffer' between Sir Hugh's artistic requirements and keeping costs down to a reasonable – though still high – level proved a mighty difficult assignment. On more than one occasion Sir Hugh 'reported' me to the Chairman for 'interference', but happily Sir Donald backed me!

Concurrently with all this it had been decided that P&O had to have a face-lift, involving the contractual appointment of a PR Consultant, Prince Yurka Galitzine, together with a common styling expert to re-design our logo and every item of P&O literature, from letter headings through advertising material to memorandum pads, bills of lading and tickets. Supervision of this exercise and the general PR of the company was given to me.

The situation within P&O at the highest level was both interesting and rather political. The charming and gentle (though very inwardly tough) Sir William – 'Willie' – Currie was still Chairman. He loved the position and was renowned for his kindness to staff, ashore and afloat. He had led a charmed life, becoming the Burra Sahib of Mackinnons Calcutta, and a GBE for his period as Chairman of the Bengal Chamber of commerce. The period as Senior Partner of McKinnons' also afforded great wealth, as the 'Partners' were extravagantly rewarded – as was the firm – by commission paid on the gross (*not* net) earnings of the BI fleet (160-plus ships) under their management plus of course earnings from agency business. So Willie was able to live in a beautiful mansion (Dinton Hall in Buckinghamshire), fully staffed with butler and footmen and other retainers. It was stated, and I do not think it was apocryphal, that Lady (Ruth) Currie had never in her life boiled an egg. One tough period for Sir William had been a Board dissension in the 1930's when he had needed to see off the aspirations of competitors in a battle for the Chair of the great company.

There were two Deputy Chairmen, my hero Donald Anderson, of whom much more later, and Viscount Simon, son of the pre-war Chancellor of the Exchequer etc. Gilbert Simon was a superbly intelligent man and one of the few in my experience who never failed to get to the point of a problem. He was gifted with a marvellously clear mind and his only shortcoming, if that is the word, was his shyness, which could be mistakenly taken for coolness and lack of empathy. 'Jimmy' Simon, the Viscountess was, by contrast, a

The Winslow Boy. *1952*

person of vagueness, artistic temperament and exuberant warmth of personality. As a consequence the Simons' cocktail parties were wonderful fun and renowned for their interesting parade of guests. I remember Ralph Richardson, Richard Baker (the ex-newsreader and later BBC music expert), Margot Fonteyn, plus all the 'greats' of the City and particularly Shipping, mingling happily at such an event. I think I got to know the Simons particularly well early on because of my performance in *The Winslow Boy*, a production of the P&O Dramatic Society. Incidentally, although I did one or two 'star' amateur dramatic performances at school and subsequently, I never really wanted to keep it up. It sounds appalling and self-acclamatory but I found acting extraordinarily easy and I was, let's face it, unusually good. I have never considered it to be other than the least admirable of artistic talents (i.e. you are either good or not and despite RADA or other 'schools' it is something that cannot really be taught). I am amazed at the Honours showered upon actors.

However, I digress.

The Chairman and Deputy Chairman were backed by an executive Board, the most prominent of whom were the Joint Managing Directors Michael Thwaites and Andrew Crichton.

And what a contrasting pair were these! Michael Thwaites was a tallish austere man with little or no sense of humour whose approach to his work and Management was that of a nit-picking examiner. With neither charisma nor charm he gloried in the niceties of the conference system (he was a long-time Chairman of the then powerful Far Eastern Freight Conference: FEFC) but he supplied no leadership and appeared to have no real understanding of the commercial money-making side of Shipping. I never heard him come up with an original idea but he was stupendously adept at rubbishing those of others. It will be apparent that I found him utterly frustrating as a boss and I was, uniquely, at odds with Sir Donald's summation of him as 'the finest world operator of Freight Liner Shipping' (said in his oration at Thwaites' Memorial Service following the latter's untimely early death).

Andrew Crichton could not have been a greater contrast. Energetic, superficial, amusing, irreverent, unashamedly self-seeking describe him best. Those characteristics obviously meant that he could not stand Michael Thwaites ('The Major' as he referred to him since he, Andrew, had been a wartime Colonel)! The feud between the two was continuing and, to my mind, disgraceful and many of us wondered why Sir Donald as Chairman allowed such a childish 'spat' to persist. Maybe he thought that a 'Divide and Rule' situation kept everyone, including the sparring duo, on their toes. Both were certainly in awe of him as Chairman. As a man I liked Andrew though he too was near impossible to work for, so quixotic were his working methods. He was moreover the personification of the legendary 'Vicar of Bray'.

This then was my working environment back at Head Office.

A major event occurred in 1959. *Oriana* was nearing completion at Vickers Armstrongs, Barrow and it became clear to the Orient Board that they were going to find it hard to raise the money for the final payment. The company was 'managed' by Anderson Green, a concern owned by the Anderson and Geddes families, as were the majority of Orient shares. The solution proposed by Sir Donald and the P&O Board was to buy out the outstanding Orient shares (by a *very* generously priced offer) and simply bring the two companies P&O and Orient under one Head (P&O-Orient) and absorb the Directors and Management. 'A merge not a swallow' was the description applied to it by Sir Austin 'Toby' Anderson, the Orient Line Chairman. Indeed it was, and a pretty shattering one for the P&O staff. The Orient Fleet consisted of some seven passenger ships.

Oriana, Orsova, Oronsay, Orcades, the old *Orion* and *Orontes* plus the tanker *Charente,* against the 60 or 70 of P&O. For this 'merge', Orient supplied a 'Management' (top brass) of no fewer than ten Directors and General Managers plus a mass of various Departmental Heads (General Freight Manager etc etc etc). It was top heavy to say the least. To cap it all no fewer than four were immediately promoted to the P&O SN Co. Group Board and the rest Directors or General Managers of the two P&O-Orient Companies. They came in at the top level and in some instances above the heads of people like myself who had joined and been trained in the big company. 'Why the big fuss? It's really only a very little company,' mused Sir William Currie the recently retired Chairman.

It was a lesson in how *not* to do a merger. Old loyalties of the Orient personnel were allowed to continue and prosper, so keen was everyone to avoid bruising their susceptibilities. The Orient team really knew only one skill, which was to run passenger ships. The sight of Michael Thwaites sharing an office with Ford Geddes, the feebly equipped cousin of Sir Donald, and now a full Managing Director of P&O, was something to behold.[1]

The only major visible change, apart from overcrowding on the Management floor, was the decision to paint the previously corn-coloured hulls of the Orient ships white like their P&O sisters. Even this decision was long delayed and fussed over! The dilettante style of various of my new colleagues annoyed me daily, but somehow had to be endured. I am sure that the sight of all this made a profound impression on the slim line Management of the BI company who were running in their Aldgate building some hundred – admittedly smaller – cargo-passenger and cargo ships plus troop ships and East Africa run passenger ships. They were to have their 'revenge' some years later.

---

[1] My description of the Orient Merge does on re-reading appear small-minded and bitter. But I am bound to say that it describes accurately how I felt. I had – as I thought – been selected for training towards a fast-track move to the main Board. A major feature of this training had been firmly pointed out to me on joining and that was to succeed *spectacularly* in three consecutive appointments in the Far East. The commitment to a 'sentence' of four years away from home was something expected of the tiny band of P&O 'Learners' in view of the prize awaiting them.

The arrival on the scene of a mass of reasonably agreeable but very different, and sometimes not very competent or experienced Directors/Managers of the small Orient Line completely changed both the current working environment and apparently promotion prospects. Most were either 'family' or the sons of good friends of the Andersons and Geddes.

At the time I felt thoroughly short changed!

Oriana was duly delivered. Her trials showed her to be a true ocean greyhound and she achieved a run of over 30 knots. There was a lot of innovative style in her interior, such gems as a John Piper mural of astonishing beauty, which I suppose was to be expected since Sir Colin Anderson an aesthete of great taste was overseeing such special artefacts.

The remainder of the ship including her grotesque profile was under the guiding hand of Ford Geddes.

1961 saw the delivery of *Canberra*. Being responsible for introducing her I, and the publicity team, had come up with the slogan 'The Ship of the Century'. When I put this to Sir Donald he charmingly but flatly (and I think absolutely correctly when one recalls the many magnificent vessels of the late Twentieth Century) turned down the suggestion. We came up with a much better idea: 'The Ship that Shapes the Future'. This was supremely appropriate because '*Canberra*'s profile embodying engines and funnel aft had been preceded only by Shaw Savill's much smaller *Southern Cross* and her very beautiful shape was to be the trail blazing template for the dozens of major cruise liners which were to follow.

I was surprised indeed but very happy when Sir Donald asked me to accompany him and Lady Anderson and one daughter Lindsay on the round-the-world maiden voyage. Although loveable in most ways, *Canberra* did have some real teething problems. Harland & Wolff had the reputation of building a 'heavy' ship and indeed *Canberra* was just this and resulted in having a 34ft draft; this was partly improved by removing her stern anchor and planting some hundreds of tons of permanent concrete ballast in the forepeak. Her second problem which affected her/us on her maiden voyage was that of leaking boiler tubes, which occasioned slower speed and a protracted delay in Aden. This meant that we were late at *every* port on the maiden voyage, occasioning some grey hairs for me as we had pre-arranged celebrations at every port en route. Dignitaries affected were such as the Governor General and Prime Minister of Ceylon/Sri Lanka.

Dame Pattie Menzies, the ship's Godmother, who was joining us in Fremantle, together with Sir Robert the Australian Prime Minister, the Mayors of Wellington and Auckland, the Governor and Mayor of Honolulu/Hawaii, the Governor of California and Mayors of Los Angeles and San Francisco, to name just a selection. All had to be re-addressed giving the 'new' dates.

We had a great welcome in San Francisco. The Chairman's party was driven through the cleared streets with a 12-motorcycle police escort. An experience indeed. Sir Donald himself was greeted by the doorman at the hotel with the words 'This way, Your Majesty!' Sir Donald winked at me, saying, *sotto voce*, 'This is a promotion I did not expect!'

My friend Jimmy Wild was however Commodore Captain and we were able to laugh out our problems with the spirited help of 'Sammy' Warren, the diminutive but marvellously good humoured and hard working Chief Purser. Jimmy Wild was, amongst all his other attributes, a great ship handler, '*Canberra*'s big foible is that she hates turning corners' was Jimmy's only criticism of his ship.

It was a splendid voyage with all sorts of interesting excursions, e.g. to Canberra with Bob Menzies where, in his office, he pointed to Perth in Western Australia on a large wall map and then traced a line along the coast up to Darwin in the Northern Territories. 'How many people, Son, do you think live in all those thousands of miles?' I had no idea, and said so. 'Well the answer is 27,000' he said. That amazing fact encapsulates the worry of Australia then and even today when Australia sits adjacent to the teeming millions of Indonesia and Malaysia. It is why also Australia is so sensitive to the problem of potential asylum seekers. Australians fear they could be so quickly overrun.

Sir Donald and I also went up to Broken Hill and down the mine there in which toil miners earned their envied 'lead bonus' miles underground. No 'outsiders' had access to this privilege. Both Australia and New Zealand were very different then from today. The 'Six o'clock swill', signified the end of drinking for the day and the sight of hundreds of red-blooded Cobbers lining up and sinking 6 or 8 large schooners of beer before staggering back into the street was pretty daunting.

The quaint liquor laws in Australia and New Zealand created other bizarre behaviour. I remember dining with the P&O No. 1 in Auckland (actually from the NZS Co.) and keeping our wine decanted into a teapot under the table which we quaffed from teacups!

The same applied to eating habits. The great influx of European immigrants had not yet happened. 'Dinner' was immutably timed for 7 o'clock (latest) and steak & eggs was the dominant fare. The unsurpassed beauty of for instance Sydney (as yet sans Opera House) was there but its emergence as one of the finest eating cities in the world was yet to happen. The extraordinary influence of Italians and Greeks in particular in the culinary area has been profound.

The voyage home was less eventful, in terms of Canberra's mechanical problems, and thus extremely enjoyable. The Andersons were marvellous travelling companions and the officers of *Canberra* performed magnificently throughout. Another feature was the chance to visit all the P&O offices en route. Those in Australia in particular were developing a desire for greater independence from Head Office, which, in terms of business generated there, was not surprising. Their aspirations had however to be treated with considerable tact.

Arriving back at Southampton we were greeted in particular by Michael Thwaites looking, if possible, more lugubrious and gloomy than normal. He had come to report to the Chairman that, during our prolonged absence, the trading figures for the Group had deteriorated and it looked like being a pretty bad year. It wasn't the best homecoming news.

In fact later in the year various cost-savings were introduced including the cancelling for that year of the long established staff Christmas Bonus.

The 'Bonus' was in fact a silly anomaly because it had become in the minds of all just regular salary with no incentive value. In order that Staff should not feel 'victimized' the Management, who did not have a bonus, had a letter from Sir Donald advising that we would be having a salary *reduction* of some 10 per cent! This is surely in sharp contrast to what has been happening in 2002/3 in the city where Directors who have occasionally put their companies into free fall with vast losses have nevertheless been 'rewarded' with bonuses/severance deals worth millions!

A major feature of 1962 in the family was the marriage of Brother Roy. Somewhat under pressure from his new and pretty wife, Sylvia, predictably a theatre sister at the Middlesex, he accepted a consultant's post in the Cheltenham Group of Hospitals and rather left the regular family circle.

The following year for me started and ended very unhappily.

It was a viciously cold winter and in January Malcolm Millar collapsed and died when clearing snow outside his house in Weybridge. This was a major blow to me, losing a wonderful boss and friend. Almost on the same day *Canberra* suffered a catastrophic electrical fire in her engine room. A junior engineer had noticed an irregularity on the main switchboard and, without consulting higher authority, had opened the switchboard and manually pulled out a circuit breaker. The result was a 9ft diameter arc generating such heat that everything in the immediate and highly sensitive area simply *melted*. Neither the young man nor anyone else was, miraculously, hurt. But *Canberra* was. Deprived of her turbo-electric propulsion she was left drifting in semi-darkness near Malta. She limped into Malta but straightway it became necessary to arrange the onward travel for *Canberra*'s stranded passengers. The answer was to put into place the biggest airlift since the famous Berlin one. Andrew Crichton was, somewhat comically, put in charge, assisted by a team led by Freddie Laker and consisting of me and many hastily assembled heroes from the passenger department. It was a crazy weekend. Planes had to be found relatives advised, 'compensation' agreed, the press informed and appeased, etc etc. One lady insisted that a radio message should be sent to her *dog* who was travelling in a cargo ship (we did not carry dogs on the passenger ships) informing him of her enforced change of plans! Had he been with us Malcolm Millar would have been in charge and spared us the 'Bluebottle' antics of Andrew Crichton, who was in a permanent state of excitement. It was typical of the 'luck' that Jimmy Wild was famous for that he had retired the previous voyage and Leslie Hill, a delightful, gentlemanly man, was now in command of *Canberra*.

I shall never forget the whole business, which somehow went off without serious incident.

Perhaps this is moment to pause and reflect on the other P&O 'Learners'. Preceding me were four. Peter Parry, son of Captain (later Sir Edward) Parry, the Captain of *Achilles* at the Battle of the River Plate against *Graf Spee*. He was a six-foot-six old Etonian who took a Double First in Classics at Cambridge. An ideal career should have been as headmaster of a boys' preparatory school. He went far in P&O. Philip Whitcombe, a charming Wykehamist, also six foot six, was a very good Oxford Blue Cricketer who had the distinction of clean bowling Sir Donald Bradman on the latter's last tour. On his way back in *Stratheden* from Bombay following his time in the East, Philip met and subsequently married the daughter of Lord Clydesmuir, the last Governor of Bombay. He left P&O on his return and this was a loss.

Keith Reynolds was one who most emphatically did stay the course. He had a razor-sharp commercial mind and was indeed a hard 'liver' (meaning life-style rather than the organ . . . though the latter might be equally apposite). Nights out on continental freight tours were something to remember (or forget!). He and I worked long together and he and his wife became firm friends. He rose, via the Board of P&O Lines, to be Managing Director of OCL. He met a sad, and horribly premature, death in the 1970s when he went scuba diving in Honolulu when breaking his journey home after a strenuous tour of the East and Australia New Zealand. I never knew if this accident was due to equipment failure or to an over-strenuous approach to scuba diving on his own part. Certainly he had not dived for years before this incident. We had been a good team when running the freight side between 1968. Those were the years when we revitalized our Liner Services. Three fast cargo ships were ordered from Mitsui Tamano yard. The idea was to run this trio, *Strathardle, Strathbrora* and *Strathconon* on 90-day round voyages non-stop UK/ continent to Japan. The service was an instant success and was implemented via an intensive Marketing plan and activity. We encouraged an energetic team in Japan who regularly visited and assisted importers as well as shippers (exporters). The same applied to Europe where our previous agents, the slightly sleepy group subsidiary General Steam, were replaced in Germany by Mareschiff- ahrtskontor, a new company set up by us, with Wolfgang Buschorn as its excellent and fearsomely aggressive and efficient boss.

Things were going swimmingly with our 'Strath' Service until we were struck by the hammer-blow of a second closure of the Suez Canal. We surely could not maintain our 90-day schedule if we had to route via the Cape until it occurred that the solution was to route via Panama. 'If the front door is shut then go round the back' was the snappy slogan that we put about with advertising and leaflets. We were the first in this competitive trade to do this (Blue Funnel Glen, Ben Line, NYK, Mitsui-OSK were all operating ships of equal quality) and we were rewarded with record earnings voyage after voyage. Success is a great incentivizor and all engaged in running the service ashore and afloat worked with mission-like zeal. With a marvellous team I used to make 10-day sorties into Germany where our supporters (always with wives . . . a special innovation!) were entertained with unforgettable parties. I always returned to the UK considerably battered after these events. Even Michael Thwaites was I seem to remember known on one occasion to congratulate the team.

But there were personal worries and changes that intruded during the early sixties quite distinct from my total involvement in P&O. I had in November 1963 been for the weekend to stay with Sir Donald and Lady Anderson in Gloucestershire. As was my wont I phoned home on Sunday evening to hear from my very concerned mother that my father had suffered an apparent stroke on Saturday. He had just been moved to the local hospital. I hurried down to Dovercourt and found father only slightly compos mentis and with only short periods of mental lucidity. I felt overwhelmingly sad and concerned for my mother, for whom this was a totally unexpected blow. Losing a parent is a unique experience and leaves a gap that is never filled. My kind and modest father was not a demonstrative man and to that extent we had never been specially close, probably because in a lot of ways we were rather alike (not the 'modest' bit, possibly!) but that did not mean that I did not love him dearly.

There seemed very little I could do – Roy was totally involved in Cheltenham with the immediately anticipated birth of Caroline his first child – so after a day or so I returned to London, and work, coming back at the weekend to continue the vigil. Later the following week came the news that he had died. This sad loss had a profound effect on my personal life over the following decade and beyond. Roy was during those following years somewhat estranged from the family. My mother and Sylvia, Roy's wife, did not 'get on'. Roy chose not unnaturally to support Sylvia right or wrong, so equally understandably, I was left, alone, to look after my mother who was herself in only moderate health. It is a frequent topic of semi-derision to talk of 'mummy's boys' who find themselves the last bastion to care for their widowed mothers. On the contrary I submit that it is an awesome responsibility embodying unique emotional ties. On the whole everything went very well though the situation must have exasperated the succession of delightful girl friends I had over the period. I used to phone my mother every day and drive down to Dovercourt most weekends, and this continued for nine years. I took her, and frequently two or three of her widowed sisters, on holidays, cruising on P&O ships. I do not regret those years but they did place a huge emotional burden on me, and with absolutely no

Jim 'fixing it' on Oriana, *with my Mother (on Jimmy's right), and aunts*

help from my brother. I do not blame him, because he had his own family concerns. It was just one of those things.

For the P&O Group as a whole the sixties were interesting years. Strategic moves were made including a decision to move into the Bulk Trades. Several of the leading Group Companies, notably P&O itself. BI and Orient were encouraged to build and operate tankers, while Hain, the previous only Group operator of 'Tramp' ships (single deck 10,000 dwt vessels), started to build bulk carriers of 40,000 dwt upward. The operation of tankers by individual companies was inefficient and tanker operations was soon consolidated under the name Trident Tankers. Chairman of Trident Tankers was nominated as Lord (Ross) Geddes, who had experience with Shell, and he in turn selected as Chief Executive my former friend A.B. ('Sandy') Marshall who emerged from an anonymous position within BI.

The development of cruising in Miami prompted by Knut Kloster greatly abetted by the ambitious former Coastguard Rear Admiral Stephens, now Chief Executive of Miami's Dodge Island Port, was growing exponentially in the Caribbean. Until then we in P&O Lines had been extending our activities initially by introducing 'circle Pacific' itineraries on the line voyages and later by operating cruises from Sydney Australia and San Francisco with voyages to Alaska, Mexico and Hawaii (the latter via Vancouver in order not to contravene the Jones Act which designated the Hawaiian Islands as being part of the US Coastline!) European Cruising was also increased.

All this was somewhat remarkably achieved using existing ships which were built for very different trades (i.e. the trunk routes to Australia and the Far East). But those basic trades had been rapidly eroded by the introduction of advanced large aircraft such as the acclaimed 'Whispering Giant' Bristol Britannia and the Lockheed Electra. These turbo props were in turn soon rapidly displaced by the first generation big jets the Boeing 707 and Douglas DC8. With the introduction of the latter the fate of the ocean liner as a primary vehicle of long distance transport was sealed, first on the transatlantic express route and very soon afterwards on all other routes.

Two very special people should be mentioned in relation to all this. First there was Keith Geddes, the younger brother of Ford. He had been a distinguished and dashing wartime night-fighter pilot (DFC), and also captained Cambridge University and Scotland Rugby sides at full back. He had a delightful manner and also possessed a creative lateral-thinking mind. He was very much responsible for the Pacific initiative and also was due much credit for encouraging the engagement of the Marine Manager of Theo H. Davies, our Agents in Hawaii, to act as the President of P&O-Orient Lines in San Francisco. This latter man was Warren Titus, still one of my dearest and admired friends, who over the years became a legend and doyen of the cruise industry. Warren had, indeed still has at 90, a charm and charisma that overwhelmed all . . . particularly the ladies.

I had two separate jobs during that time. The 'Group' one was to act as 'Corporate Affairs Director' though without that more recently accepted description. It was a fascinating and very necessary portfolio, the main and only danger being that one became very high profile, which inflamed jealousy among many colleagues. I was so devoted to the job and the need to change P&O and present it to best advantage to the world that I was curiously, perhaps naively, unaware of such undercurrents.

Our agents in Australia – The company of P&O Australia Ltd, the combination of MacDonald Hamilton and Orient Line Australia – were experiencing some bad press particularly at the hands of the young Rupert Murdoch and his *Australian*, the very first newspaper which covered all of Australia rather than the individual states and their capital cities. This broad coverage was achieved by printing in Canberra and flying the copies in a small fleet of Dakota Aircraft during the night.

Sir Donald asked me to go to Australia to endeavour to correct the situation. This I undertook and brought with me Peter Thomas, our able Press Officer of the time whom I had engaged some few years before.

The nub of the Murdoch criticism was that the 'lordly' P&O was squeezing the profits of Australian industry, particularly the farmers, a 'grumble of graziers' being the collective noun given to them by Viscount Slim when he was Governor General.

I can still recall a long meeting in Canberra with the great though still young Murdoch. His door remained open throughout so I assumed he could keep an eye on the other open door of the Editor. The latter was fired at very regular intervals!

The problem was finally solved by our appointing a Press Officer, a professional, who had recently returned from the Australian High Commission in London. The fault had been that the Directors of P&O Australia were extraordinarily reluctant to even talk to the press – thinking them to be no more than a destructive element – and the press concluded on their part that the whole organization was therefore pompous and antipathetic. A friendly Press Officer was able gradually to win over most of them – including RM. This was in about 1965.

My second P&O Lines job, latterly as a Director, was in three separate periods to be in charge of marketing first the passenger ships, second the Freight Liner Services and then, again the passenger ships' cruising after their Liner Services had been abandoned. 'Marketing' was not a word familiar to my senior colleagues (Thwaites once referred it as 'Gobbledygook') so its introduction was no easy task.

The great liner shipping transformation that took place in the sixties was of course the sudden – and it was dramatically sudden –

introduction of 'Containerization'. The American Malcolm MacLean who originally was a trucking man had turned to the Sea as a transport supplier to the Vietnam War. His fleet, called Sealand, became available for other employment at the conclusion of hostilities so he introduced a commercial transatlantic service. The shock waves from this quickly alerted the established owners as they saw the rapid erosion of their centuries-old trades. Over a dinner at, I seem to recall, Brooks's club, the Chairmen of the major ship owning Groups, P&O, Ocean, Furness and British-Commonwealth sat down and sketched out the formation of a joint company, Overseas Containers Limited, 'OCL', to take over the previously operated conventional liner trades. It meant that trades had to be allocated (i.e. the P&O Group organization ran the Australian trade, while ocean-through Swires, their old Agents, dominated the Far East trades etc etc).

The allocations were pretty rough and ready, but it was felt, probably correctly, that something had to be done *fast*. Busy little Andrew Crichton was made Chairman of OCL, and Directors, (largely drawn from the constituent companies and including my old workmate Keith Reynolds of P&O) were appointed.[2]

About this time Michael Thwaites sadly suffered a fatal heart attack in the train from Weybridge on his way to the office. Peter Parry whom I have already described was appointed Chairman of P&O Lines. It was a case of nit-picking being replaced by wobbling indecision and resulted in the Passenger Shipping activity going to a very low place in the competition for the Group's capital allocation. This was particularly significant because the Bulk activity – tankers above all, was going through one of its customary booms – and Mr A.B. (Sandy) Marshall, its executive Head, was not slow in pointing out that his mini-empire should have priority. (His case he strongly backed by his assessment of his own judgement and management rather than the simple good fortune of the short-term cycle.)

After interminable research under the leadership of the Project Director of P&O Lines it was finally decided to purchase on the

---

[2]On reflection it is quite astonishing that owners did not recognize the need to do something much earlier. For years the Dockers had made the running of cargo liners hopelessly difficult. Strikes were frequent, frivolous stoppages almost daily (e.g. awards of 'temptation money' demanded for handling whisky in cases, or 'embarrassment money' for handling lavatory pans (unpacked) etc etc). Pilferage was rampant not just in the UK but also in destination ports. The introduction of Containers thus meant that transits were vastly improved, time in port was dramatically reduced and pilferage was largely eliminated.

stocks from Fincantieri a new building originally ordered by Norwegian Caribbean as, I think projected *Southward*. She was a nice little design (some 16,000 GRT) through nothing special as a great leap forward for P&O. London was the 'in' place of the period so *Spirit of London* was her chosen name and the Pearly Queen her lady sponsor. The trouble with the whole episode was that for our first-ever speciality designed cruise ship we went for a small, second-hand design short-range vessel, an appalling reflection on our management dynamism and forward planning.[3] An amusing event had been when I went with my colleague Projects Director Sandy Stirling (very ex-Orient Line) to Miami to undertake personal research of the new cruising explosion. We sailed in *Song of Norway* then RCCL's only ship. I still smile when I think of Sandy Stirling going round furrow-browed with a tape measure recording cabin sizes, while I felt it more relevant and certainly more enjoyable to experience the entertainment/ambience side of things and succeeded in achieving the vote as the (totally phoney) dance champion of the ship.

On that trip I went to see Mr Ted Arison, then with NCL, who accused P&O/me of 'stealing' his ship design. He was so abrupt that I replied with equal asperity that he should remember that I represented the world's greatest shipping company and accordingly he should temper his language (which he did!) In view of later events (i.e. son Mickey Arison has now with his company Carnival taken over P&O Cruises, Cunard Holland, America etc) that conversation has almost legendary significance! 'What a falling off was there.'

Sir Donald retired in 1971 and Ford Geddes took over.[4]

---

[3] The ordering of this little ship was an even greater criticism of the then Board. Everyone on it seemed beguiled by the then success of the new Bulk Shipping Division which was going through one of that activity's periods of great success and profitability. Surely it was apparently assumed this is where the Group's capital should be directed. Mr A. B. (Sandy) Marshall an opportunist as ever took full advantage of this state of mind. I was appalled by the Board's inability to realize that cruising was on the very brink of entering the most spectacular growth period of maritime or indeed any other industry.

[4] The retirement of Donald Anderson had indeed been a sad day for me. He was an Olympian figure but graced with a great sense of humour and formidable intellect. His fault so far as I saw it was in the selection of his close advisers. He leant heavily on Sir Fredric (Freddie) Harmer, the Deputy Chairman of P&O, and Chairman of the NZS Co. 'Freddie' was a self-acclaimed mathematical genius (in *Who's Who* he carefully set out his 1st Class Honours and Senior Wrangler status at Cambridge). This facility with figures did not however allow him to realize that sending large fully crewed (300-odd) passenger/cargo ships such as *Rangitiki, Rangitane, Remuera* etc on voyages entailing several months on the New Zealand Coast waiting for the various wool and meat sales was not particularly clever or profitable scheduling.

The saga of the Thwaites/Crichton feud I have already described.

Sir Donald's last and most significant personnel ill judgement was however his selection of Ford

Things certainly started to happen in 1972. The MacKinsey boys were making their bruising way through all Departments of the company. It was somewhat mesmeric to be faced with one of these young investigators in one's office and be asked 'And what do you do?' Just like that.

I was extraordinarily busy marketing the passenger ships and trying, despite the enervating performance of Peter Parry, to look to its future.

We had with Stephan Schoor our Marketing/PR consultant covering Europe a major 'Do' in Amsterdam to launch our continental cruising season. 'Miss Amsterdam' was there to glamorize the occasion when we literally launched a cardboard boat into a pool of water. Miss A was however totally out-classed by one of our Dutch Women Assistant Pursers who was there in uniform as part of the team; her name Hanny Verhoef.

Hanny had become interested in a life at sea by seeing on Dutch NCR television a programme called 'Gevraagd' (literally 'Wanted'). It was hosted by the late Godfrey Bowmans, the most popular presenter on Dutch Television. He was more than just a presenter, being an

---

Geddes his cousin, as his successor as Chairman. Beetle-browed Ford was likeable, that is apart from a somewhat pompous patronizing manner . . . but he possessed virtually no 'chairman-required' skills. He loved the minutiae of Passenger Ship operation – the softness of chair seats, the cleanliness of cabins and galleys etc etc – but with no visible strategic ideas. While still a Managing Director he presided over a committee that I had managed to inspire to endeavour to rationalize certain things under a Group – as opposed to individual Company – logo. Take for instance coat hangers. Some of the smaller Companies baulked at losing their much-loved names from these items. Ford's Solomon-like decision was therefore not to impose 'P&O Group' on these objectors, but instead go for 'Shipco'! This decision totally missed the point and was thus meaningless and pointless. It illustrated however an important example of Ford Geddes' management technique, which in so short a while accelerated his fall from power. He was Chairman for just over one catastrophic year.

In retrospect it was ironic that it was I as 'Corporate Affairs' Director (though no such high flown title then existed) who had just prior to Sir Donald's retirement recommended to him that the whole structure of the P&O Group, with its 100 plus companies each with its own Chairman, Board, Finance Director Secretary etc, should be looked at by a consultancy company. It fell to Ford Geddes to follow this up and, characteristically, he gave McKinsey's a totally free hand and no clear indication of what he was expecting of them. The outcome was a wholesale destruction of morale as the twenty-plus-year-old lads sent in as 'consultants' made their bruising progress through every Company and Department.

To my mind the incontrovertible rule when employing a consultant such as MacKinsey is to let them know exactly what you are seeking from them and to keep them and their actions under firm control. A 'free hand' such as was given them in P&O led to a major loss of morale and self-esteem among employees ashore and afloat.

It is perhaps interesting to note that while under this MacKinsey exercise all companies of the Group were centralized and split only into 'Divisions' (Dry Cargo Division, Passenger Division etc etc), when Jeffrey Sterling and his team came to power they reinstated individual companies and Boards . . . though very many fewer than pre-1972.

eccentric, philosopher, writer and original thinker. It had been contrived (by the energetic Stephan Schoor) that on this most popular of programmes P&O should choose from a number of girl applicants a Dutch WAP.

The programme was a roaring success and I appeared as one of the three examiners with Godfrey and Guus Oster, a prominent Dutch actor. To cut a long story short Hanny, who had seen the programme, later applied for the job. whether attracted by the seagoing prospect or the sight of me I dare not conjecture. You will gather that later she became my wife! (And incidentally would emphatically say that it *was* the seagoing prospect that lured her to P&O!)

However we were not too successful with our continental Europe cruising. I had appointed Wolfgang Buschhorn's company, Mare Schiffahrtskontor, as our passenger general agents after their spectacular success on the freight side with the new 'Straths'. But the continental, especially German, cruising market was at a very early stage of development, much different from the UK. Also our ships were far from ideal. We stationed the *Chitral* (former CMB *Jadotville*) in Genoa. She was a comfortable passenger/cargo vessel but neither large enough in amenities or indeed passenger numbers to be profitable. But she was a learning process for P&O in catering for continental passengers and developing the fly-cruise concept from the UK.

We were also planning to cruise *Canberra* from New York where Home Lines were doing very well with their not dissimilar *Oceanic*.

With all this going on I certainly was too occupied to notice the shifting sands beneath my feet being created by the little men of MacKinseys. At the end of the year however I accidentally came across a memorandum from MacKinsey's to Peter Parry setting out a new passenger organization. I asked Parry what he thought of it and, incidentally, where I personally fitted in. He blushed, and stammering even more than usual – he was afflicted lifelong with a major stutter – said:

'W-w-w-well Jim that has to be decided and m-m-maybe you will go elsewhere in the Group.' I could not believe my ears. I, not alone I know, had been propping up Parry's sorry leadership for years and was now being unceremoniously 'dumped' with his passive acquiescence, the post of Global Marketing Director having been scrapped. Also, with mass redundancies in all senior areas, there was precious little prospect of being greeted elsewhere in the Group.

At this exact time Ford Geddes heavily advised by two non-executive Board Members from Lazards, Lord (Oliver) Poole and 'Denny' Marris came up with the brilliant – he thought – scheme of 'merging' P&O with Bovis (the property developers and house builders). It was, it was alleged, an almost mystical combination of an undercapitalized fast-moving profitable company (Bovis) with a sleepy low-profitable cash rich company (P&O). In fact it meant giving away the great P&O on totally unsatisfactory terms. The proposal even contained the astonishing proposal that Frank Sanderson the CEO of Bovis should become CEO of the combined Group with Ford Geddes serenely sitting on top as Chairman!

The 'Merge' was doomed to failure and rapidly the Earl of Inchcape and Mr. A.B. (Sandy) Marshall – the latter seeing his big chance – supported by two other nondescript recently joined Executive Directors, D.D. Brown (from the Foreign Office) and Cliff Nancarrow (from I think British Oxygen) came out as dissenters to the whole deal.

While not able to do much overtly myself I quietly backed Marshall and his strange group and Marshall even made a phone call from my house in Campden Street to Sir Donald which resulted in Sir Donald writing a letter to *The Times* condemning the proposed merger. 'P&O is not a beached whale.' This was a decisive act, and a very difficult one for Sir Donald, because he was effectively putting the skids under his cousin and personal appointee, Ford. A few days later at an Extraordinary General meeting Ford and most of the Board resigned.

I mention all this in rather more detail than befits my story because this extraordinary series of events resulting in victory for my erstwhile friend Marshall would I thought mean that my own position in the P&O whether or not in Passenger Division could and would be reassessed. But when I had a word with the now all-powerful Marshall he merely said 'A bit difficult, Jim, things seem to have gone so far! And you have had such a superb job offer' (with KB). Needless to say incidentally Parry, despite throughout holding up his hand in support of the Bovis deal, had *not* resigned and was clinging on to his seat for dear life, as were such as Andrew Crichton, Harry Beazley, Dick Adams and McNaughton Sidey. It was not an edifying sight. Rapidly Marshall as Managing Director, under Inchcape as Executive Chairman, set about establishing his new team. For the time being

Adams, Parry, Beazley, Sidey and Nancarrow remained in charge of their respective Divisions. No former P&O Lines Director gained a prominent role. All the key appointments came from Marshall's own former company, the BI. I viewed this, now from afar, with astonishment. Poor Marshall would have been equally astonished when all these colleagues failed to rally behind him just a few years later. He, Marshall, seemed to believe that he really had a Midas touch and seemed not to understand the frighteningly regular cycles of shipping. He subsequently published an autobiography entitled *Take the Adventure*, in which he describes himself in positively heroic terms as a person massively misunderstood, but fundamentally right in all he did. A production of some hubris.

Sandy Marshall had made the great error of alienating Andrew Crichton, the Vicar of Bray personality, who had stuck like glue to the P&O Board and had become Inchcape's confidant and closest adviser. Andrew certainly knew how to hate and he lost no opportunity to criticise Marshall's investment thrust which early was showing signs of dragging down the annual result. To cut it short, a coup was organized and the hapless Marshall found himself without any support from his self-described 'Dream Team'. He modestly chronicled this in his memoirs 'I had lost my company'. Others I might have reminded him had felt the same at his hands. Another thing worth quoting from his memoirs was that on completing his year as President of The General Council of British Shipping he had declined the offer of a CBE. His reason, 'I could not see the merit of accepting the honour simply for doing a job.' A curious phrase.

I fear my acid feelings about both Marshall and Parry are here revealed all too clearly but each was a person I had supported with loyalty over many years and who unceremoniously let me down. Nevertheless I retained a certain pity for Sandy Marshall. Few people can have so hugely overestimated their own ability and, concurrently, gathered such a feeble 'team' around him. His fall from power engineered by Inchcape and Crichton was as complete as it was abrupt. The ensuing years for P&O I shall describe elsewhere, more appropriate since I was then an outside observer and not part of the action.

Now what? Several very good friends hearing somewhat bemusedly of my imminent departure from P&O wrote charming letters but one in particular came to me with an immediate offer. This was from

Kleinwort Benson, then the largest City Merchant Bank, in the person of Robin Fox, a Director who incidentally had married my old friend Lindsay Anderson, Sir Donald Anderson's daughter who as described had been with us on *Canberra*'s maiden voyage. Thus in the event, I had just one week off before joining KB. Also the terminal arrangements from P&O, though positively derisory when compared with today's golden 'hellos', 'goodbyes', and 'parachutes', meant that together with a very fair (slightly improved) salary from KB I had a solidly improved financial position.

But personally I was shattered at leaving P&O. In my most despairing moments it had never remotely occurred to me that I would ever leave the great company. Naively I had thought that my devotion, my conscientiousness, and my contribution had been so great that despite any 'political' consideration my position and indeed my future were unassailable. My sole ambition had been to work my whole career with P&O and ultimately achieve the position of Chairman. A self-delusion, it transpired, of positively gargantuan proportions!

Among those many letters I received was a treasured one from Sir Donald in which he professed himself completely baffled by my

With Hanny (on the left of course) at our very first meeting

'redundancy'. I had a huge selection of letters from a wide number of good friends . . . from Jimmy Saville to Lord Macpherson.

But it was a time to follow the Life Maxim of Commodore Jimmy Wild, 'Look forward not back, look up not down . . .' and this I resolved to do with total commitment.

Hanny and I became engaged shortly after I left P&O and I cannot say how much I owe her for her steadfast support during that difficult period. Young and beautiful – a whole 20 years younger than I – she resolutely took me on. I was further distracted by my mother's illness. She had an unsuccessful hip operation, which became infected, added to which she developed a form of internal cancer. The net result was that she was in the Middlesex Hospital on our Wedding Day . . . a sad, sad omission. However she did get reasonably better and survived another three years before she died in December 1976. During those years despite being much occupied with producing and weaning our first born Mariske *and* moving house, Hanny was a regular visitor to my increasingly infirm mother. I was so lucky with my belated choice of bride.

CHAPTER 7

Kleinwort Benson

KLEINWORT BENSON, its Directors and Staff, together with its positively alarming assembly of activities was a very different organization from the P&O Company. I write 'organization' and yet this, it became quickly clear to me, was the quality which KB itself somewhat lacked. There was no traditional 'coathanger' of responsibilities, but instead a collection of clever and highly qualified personalities who went about their business each with their own supporting staff. KB was thus more like a Partnership of Solicitors or Chartered Accountants than a coherent company. This in many ways was deemed essential in that there had, indeed have, to be 'Chinese Walls' between for instance the Investment Division and the Corporate Finance Division where otherwise there could exist conflict of interest and – horror of horrors – accusation of 'insider trading', nowadays a criminal offence.

My colleagues were most welcoming and I tried to overcome my confusion over how the place was actually run. I reported to the Head of Banking Division since my own duty was to institute in KB a portfolio of loans to ship-owners. This 'Ship Mortage' activity was at its very peak at the time and had been identified as a major banking opportunity that needed to be developed. (The decision to enter Shipping was made at a Board 'think tank' or 'love in' which in those years, 1971–73, was held annually at Selsdon Park Hotel.)

A special feature of KB at that time was that KB had in the last few years grown exponentially from a rather small organization, capable of being run in a 'cosy', apparently dilettante, manner into a large company that desperately needed a more rigid structure.

A delightful feature was the Directors' Luncheon Room (there were some 30 or so Directors at the time) where on a normal day a huge joint of beef or equivalent was served which each Director could approach to carve off his individual helping. That and many other little obsolescences created a charming country house atmosphere in the company. The two Kleinwort brothers Ernest and Cyril still attended but were no longer intimately involved on a day-to-day basis.

For my first years Gerald Thompson was Chairman, and Bobby Henderson then took over. Occasionally I discussed with Bobby, a superb man, my sense that the increasingly big KB was woefully lacking in structure. His startling reply was that if people needed direction then they were the wrong type to be working in KB! From such an intelligent and charming man I found this philosophy baffling.

I had thought before transferring from P&O to KB that I knew most of what there was to know about shipping. I rapidly discovered that this was far from the case. P&O at that time, still the world's largest shipping company, could be likened to a mighty VLCC ploughing through the oceans of the world. The most violent storm scarcely troubled or moved the ship while lesser vessels were being tossed and thrown around. In other words P&O to a great extent created its own environment. When I started to deal with the lesser mortals of the shipping company complex it was a very different environment. The Greeks were – they had to be! – entrepreneurial, extremely quick in decision making and mightily cost conscious. Also they were very skilful in dealing with and extracting money from, Banks. Onassis and Niarchos in particular were still building up their fleets, and fortunes, using Ship Mortgage Loans and Shipyard Credit.

In the Far East the shipping tycoons were also fast emerging in the shape of C.Y.Tung, T.Y. Chao and the most formidable, Y.K. Pao. There was a legion of lesser names also in Hong Kong. The Hong Kong owners were noticeably less risk-taking than their European counterparts and Y.K Pao developed a unique relationship with the Japanese oil and shipping companies whose *shikumisen* activity (i.e. granting very long-term pay-out [Bareboat] charters) was in fact bankable. One simply arranged the charterer, the builder, the providing bank and the owner round a table and signed simultaneously. In this way one did not have to put in any equity. For Y.K. it was a delightfully simple way of making money!

The bubble of shipping prosperity burst with a mighty pop in the October (1973) after I joined KB. The October Yom Kippur War introduced a situation when the OAPEC oil-producing nations used for the first time oil as a strategic weapon. Concurrently Sheikh Yamani the voice of the OAPEC nations was trumpeting the 'fact' that oil was a finite resource (which of course it is) which would be used up in a very few decades (which of course it would not!). The combination of these two resulted in a total collapse in tanker rates. The Bergen based Hilmar Reksten, a great player of the markets, concluded that this was another 'cyclical' setback and calmly left his entire fleet unfixed while he waited for better rates to resume. Inexorably he went bust . . . a sad demise for one who had been a swashbuckling somewhat romantic figure and prominent collector of Picassos and other modern art. His was the greatest fall but many lesser lights, particularly in Norway, were snuffed out by the market collapse. Clearly so soon after my setting up the ship finance activity in KB this situation did not exactly help my expansionist ideas. Many banks who previously had been shovelling money into ships ('floating real estate') suddenly found that their loans were significantly uncovered by the mortgage value of the ships. It produced a predictable reaction from my banking colleagues in KB whose previous appetite for shipping disappeared almost overnight. Another shock to my system!

I had always considered bankers as the top-level intelligentsia of the commercial world, but abruptly learned that – despite this undoubted intellectual superiority – they are lemming-like in their enthusiasms and hatreds. One minute they are all in favour of a certain activity (be it shipping, real estate, IT etc etc) and the next they all flee from it. This obviously makes for violent fluctuations, which, with the application of calm commonsense, could be largely avoided, or at least lessened.

We had already concluded a large two-ship deal – *shikumisen* style – with a London Greek as intermediary to Japan Lines, which greatly strained the nerve of the banking Directors. We therefore split the deal with Bank of America International – they 'leading' one ship and KB the other – and subsequently bought out the intermediary Greek, thus becoming owners through two one-ship owning companies.

In the autumn of that momentous year Hanny and I were married in a charming service in the Dutch Church in Austin Friars in the City. Hanny looked wonderful, though sadly the celebration itself had to be somewhat low-key because, as I have mentioned, my mother was seriously ill in the Middlesex Hospital following an unsuccessful hip-replacement operation. There were many friends at the wedding who gazed in disbelief at the sight of this 45-year-old bachelor uniting with a beautiful, much younger, Dutch bride. 'It won't last,' was murmured by several. But it did and here we are happy together some 33 years later, as I write. It actually surprised me the way from the date of marriage I settled instantly and with not one backward glance.

It was essentially a learning time for the maritime industries. Until 1972 shipping journalism had confined itself to rather limited reporting. There was a significant press corps including Monty Lacey of the *Express*, Jack Frost of the *Telegraph* and David Fairhall of the *Guardian*, plus the 'professionals' from *Lloyds List*, *The Motor Ship* and *Journal of Commerce*. None of these however really probed or questioned the trading activities of companies. It was more a case of reporting on the personalities (from Directors to Captains) and, through company press releases exploring technical advances and the like. But in 1972 burst on the scene *Seatrade*, a Greek-owned magazine by Themis Vokos, which really went in to the economics of shipping and mounted annual conferences entitled 'Money and Ships'. These encouraged audiences of more than 1000 in the Great Room of Grosvenor House. I think I spoke at 13 consecutive such conferences including the first Open Debate when personalities such as Sven Salen, Derek Kimber, Frank Chao and Abbas Gokal were involved. The merit of it all was that, superficially at least, the industry leaders were starting to indulge in some lateral thinking and really examining in a detached way the whole process of building and running ships. It had always been such a seductive industry that those involved (including I must admit, myself to a large degree) enjoyed it so much that they went with the flow and simply accepted 'change' in such areas as size and propulsion. The container revolution had been a unique earth shaking development (forced upon the industry as said by a trucking man). Roll-on/Roll-off (Ro-Ro) in the short sea trades was another such profound development, which completely trans-formed the efficiency and productivity of ships, which, hitherto miniature liners as they were, had like their bigger ocean-going sisters been subject to the whims and behaviour of dock workers.

I gradually recruited a lively team for KB's Shipping Department, notable among whom was a young Greek London trained accountant and a Malaysian barrister, a charming intelligent girl. The former was invaluable in introducing us/me to the younger, smaller Greek ship-owners (on whom it seemed a good idea to concentrate as niche business) and with the other well-established major owners. The Chandris Brothers were both good friends dating from my P&O

Two shipowners, the great Mimis Chandris on my left and Abbas Gokal, who later experienced some 'local problems', on my right

days, and it was a terrible blow when both died in middle age. The brothers Anthony and Dimitris had brilliantly entered the passenger ship market by buying, extremely cheaply, old displaced passenger liners. Tony entered the Australian trade with *Patris* (ex *Bloemfontein Castle*, *Amerikanis* (ex *Kenya Castle*) *Ellinis* (ex *Lurline*) and *Australis* (ex *America*). These ships became mighty competition for us in P&O but throughout possibly inflammatory negotiations we had remained great friends. Dimitris exploited, almost invented, the fly-cruise market in the Mediterranean, utilizing former cross-channel vessels like *Amsterdam* and *Duke of York*, which became *Fiorita* and *Fiesta*. Dimitris I once met on a plane flying back from New York having bought *Victoria*, ex *Dunnottar Castle* (built 1934!), from, I think, the Longshoreman's Union who had acquired the ship on the bankruptcy of Incres Line. He had paid just over $400 000 for this beautifully updated vessel which continued cruising with Chandris as *The Victoria* for another 30 years. What a buy! The brothers would surely have blinked when the next generation of John and Michael placed orders at Meyer Werft for *Horizon* and *Zenith* at some $200/300 million a time, followed by even bigger and more expensive ships.

Apart from my duties within KB, outside activities began to play an increasing part in my life throughout the seventies. I found myself increasingly in demand as a speaker at, or as chairman of, conferences. Most important of all was the founding of IMIF (the International Maritime Industries Forum) in 1975. I also became more involved in the Chartered Institute of Transport leading to my election as President in 1980.

The Chartered Institute of Transport was in those days a splendid organization. It sought the admirable aim of 'professionalism in transport' and achieved this by a combination of student teaching, leading to the achievement of a degree, MCIT, and well-aimed lobbying, not least with the Department of Transport. The greatest supporters of the CIT came from rail and road, plus rather less prominently air and sea, the latter of which I constantly sought to improve by convincing my peers in P&O and the other major players, Cunard Group, Furness Group. Ocean, B&C, Blue Star, etc, that one of the natural pathways to promotion should be by passing the Institute's exams and gaining the accolade of MCIT.

I chose as the theme of my Presidential address in 1980 'Transport . . . an under-rewarded industry', a theme I have held to ever since.

My year as President was thoroughly enjoyable and I took my duties seriously by attending most major branches' 'happenings'. Many of the latter were dinners on Friday nights involving a speech, and the only negative was waking up in a hotel in, say, Middlessbrough or Liverpool on a Saturday morning, which meant that the precious weekend was seriously shortened. An extremely valuable plus was meeting with the Chairmen of the big transport organizations like British Airways, British Rail, BRS and ABP, who in turn supplied council members and, often presidents. The Institute had a close relationship with the Secretary of State for Transport, (during my time David – now Lord – Howell) and the Permanent Secretary (then Sir Peter Baldwin followed by Sir Peter Lazarus). We worked hard at producing a UK Transport policy (this in 1980!), which is still being worked on today! We arranged some wonderful seminars with internationally renowned speakers. I shall never forget after one of these seminars, driving along the embankment with Jim Lovell, a traveller indeed as captain of Apollo 13 and 14. He was the one

*President of the Chartered Institute, with David (now Lord) Howell,
then Secretary of State for Transport, 1980*

portrayed by Tom Hanks in the film. He is an unbelievably
impressive man of modesty, sang-froid and visible calmness and
competence. We were driving home together after a reception in the
Mansion House and I had the sunshine roof open of my car. Along
the Embankment I looked up at a gorgeous full moon and it was a
positively eerie feeling to think that this charming soul alongside me
had been there, not once but twice.

I retain a very warm feeling for the 'old' CIT, and the late dear
Brigadier Donald Locke its then Director General, which has now
been subsumed into partnership with the Institute of Logistics and in
the process has lost its old atmosphere of camaraderie.

The Far East was a focal point of interest in the late seventies.
Already dominating Shipbuilding were the Japanese but then bursting
on the scene came the Koreans. Hyundai, Samsung and Daewoo built
huge Graving Docks capable of turning out vlcc's and anything
smaller in record time and in record numbers.

I annually led an IMIF team to Korea to warn them of the dangers
that lay ahead for all parties with the introduction of such a mass of

shipbuilding capacity. I remember a hilarious meeting with the President of Daewoo when as we entered the office he looked up to greet our delegation of very senior Ship-owners and Bankers. 'Ah, you have come from half-time Europe,' he cheerfully said. 'You have become fat and lazy!' I looked furtively at my team to reassure myself that he meant some others and not just myself. It was indeed a singular greeting. After hearing our views he went on to say that he had no particular problems with European yards but was definitely going to take on the Japanese. 'It is our turn now!' he enthused. I gently pointed out that this was akin to saying that one could make a great splash up one end of a swimming pool and the ripples would not affect others at the other end: they most certainly would. However he was unconvinced and went his merry way producing and selling ships at knock-down prices until the yard's losses reached such a level that he was unceremoniously removed as President of Daewoo Heavy Industries.

IMIF had its beginnings in 1975 when it was recognized that the crisis in shipping was not this time the same as the familiar cyclical 'boom and bust' that had beset the industry for years. Intense overbuilding due to unthinking optimism after the lean war and postwar years had produced a situation of '*stable* chronic oversupply' as my friend Derek Kimber, a dedicated and wonderful 'one off' shipbuilding character described it. The people who saw this most clearly were the Scandinavians, particularly the Norwegians, so many of whom had lost not only 'face' but their entire companies in this devastating slump. Reksten was the most famous but there were plenty of smaller ones who shared his fate. Jorgen Jahre, previously renowned as one of the founders of Intertanko, was a progenitor of IMIF, realizing that resolution of the crisis could not be achieved by ship-owners alone but must involve all those in the maritime activity, i.e. bankers, shipbuilders, insurers and charterers plus various governments who were interfering with the market by way of shipbuilding subsidies and the like. The person chosen to be the first chairman was redoubtable beetle-browed Whitehall Mandarin Sir James (Ned) Dunnett GCB CMG and the original advisory committee consisted of:

Shipowners	Shipbuilders	Bankers	Oil Companies
Chandris Lines A.J Chandris	Kockums N H Hallenborg	Deutsche Schiffsbank W. Behrman	CIC Française de Petroles Mr E. Dalemont
Anders Jahre Rederi Jorgen Jahre	Mitsubishi HI I Takezawa	Hambros Otto Norland	BP Tankers Ltd R.B Horton
Worldwide/ Marine Navigation H. Sohmen	A.G. Weser L. Vernede		Petrofina SA Baron Snoy
Taiheiyo KKK S. Yamaji			

Others involved in those early days were such as the great Maersk McKinney Moller and of course myself.

To chronicle my years at Kleinwort Benson in detail could be wearisome. My fellow banking directors having become somewhat fearful of financing shipping I was obliged to turn my energies elsewhere.

We already had a very good client list and with one notable exception we had had no bad debts. Loucas Hajioannou, father of the entrepreneur Stelios and of Polys, was an early client and he maintained a most commendable routine of making his Bank repayments both loan and interest several days early. I have one specially treasured memory of Loucas – now, alas, not a very well man – of one day when he came to me and asked for a $40 million loan to take over a vlcc then on the stocks building for a distressed Norwegian owner. The tanker market had already collapsed and Loucas, uniquely for him, seemed to have got his judgement all wrong, and I declined to arrange the loan. At the time he was very upset because I had always before helped him. I said 'Loucas, my view of the market is that in six months you will be able to buy that ship or another equivalent for $10 million, so don't do it now!' He didn't and he did (i.e. he later picked up another vessel for $10 million)! Loucas never forgot that experience and he has remained a

With the great Greek shipowners, Messrs Frangos and Hajioannou

dear friend ever since. Afterwards he achieved immense wealth and success in particular by running the shuttle service of tankers during the Iran/Iraq War.

He lost several ships from Exocet air attacks but with astronomical freight rates he made a fortune beyond dreams. A small portion of this he gave to his two sons, with results which all can see, particularly with the case of 'Easyjet Stelios'.

Other excellent clients were Odfjell, Lanaras, Tsourinakis, to name just a few.

The corporate financiers of KB were having a fine old time, particularly with work from the 'Privatization' initiatives of Margaret Thatcher's Government. BT was the first big one and there was heavy involvement with many others. This division of the Bank contained such luminaries as Martin Jacomb, Charles Ball, Andrew Caldecott, David Clementi and Simon Robertson. They were a talented lot but even then it struck me how quaint it was that they should be advising major companies on structure and management. None of them had experience of running a major organization, being lawyers or accountants. KB itself resembled more a partnership (of accountants or solicitors) rather than a coherent structure. However . . .

On the shipping side I put it to my colleagues that we should take a well-known shipbroking company, which had a fine name, Harley Mullion, but which had fallen on hard times.

The trouble with Harley Mullion was that 'hard times' had resulted in a defection of most of the creative staff and an almost total collapse of morale. It was therefore a case of building afresh and recruiting a new team to work under the charming but somewhat diffident Managing Director Ken Lazenby. The whole operation never really took off because it proved exceedingly difficult to recruit top-line 'rain makers'. A positive move was to set up a parallel organization in Hong Kong but there were reasons *not* to use the Harley Mullion name because Mullion had in an earlier decade departed the Colony leaving some unhappy creditors! However we went on to purchase Rodskog Shipbrokers, a team of young enthusiasts, and thereon trade as KB Shipbrokers. Meanwhile Harley Mullion in London went on to some more interesting trading by purchasing old ships, trading them for one or at most two voyages and then selling them for scrap, generally in India or Taiwan. It was by no means high quality business but made modest money in a period of perilously low freight rates.

The story of Harley Mullion was yet one more example of my banker colleagues proving unwilling to take a long term view and rapidly withdrawing interest, enthusiasm and support if things did not go stupendously well from the start. That is why banks are not well positioned to indulge in entrepreneurial activity.

When I 'retired' from KB in 1988 my colleagues lost no time in selling off the shipbroking activities in London and Hong Kong at a knock-down price. The buyers enjoyed some super-profits because the market was on the turn and uncompleted deals suddenly yielded great returns. The bank's shipping activities were concurrently slimmed to near extinction.

Nevertheless in the late seventies and throughout the eighties I had plenty of outside activities to keep me busy. I was President of the Chartered Institute of Transport in 1980–1, became Chairman of IMIF in 1981, President of the National Waterways Association in 1982, President of the Institute of Freight Forwarders in 1982, President of the Institute of Supervision and Management in 1985, President of the Institute of Chartered Shipbrokers in 1988, and President of the Institute of Export in 1993. These were of course all 'pro bono' activities as was my six-year Chairmanship of the Marine Society starting in 1987. I remain also on the Council (after some 30 years) of The Mission to Seafarers.

I think my record of the Institute Presidencies is unrivalled and unique and each one of them produced challenges of its own.

A rather less commercial presidency has been that of the World Ship Society (to which I am now contributing a *third* term). This extraordinary Society comprises the world's ship fanciers. Consisting of all shades of society from barristers and clergymen to tug masters and dockworkers, the World Ship Society was founded in the fifties by Michael Crowdy, a Chartered Surveyor from Cumbria, and it has grown and grown, encompassing overseas chapters and members. It publishes monthly its magazine *Marine News*, which has more detailed news of individual ships than any other publication I have ever seen. The ultimate vade mecum of ships.

I would summarize my 15 years with KB as a period of learning and frustration, fairly evenly distributed. I was very fortunate indeed to join such a distinguished group and enjoy some years in a totally fresh environment. It was a whole new world, but pure 'banking' (i.e. the lending of money under various guises on if possible a risk-free basis) provided limited intellectual stimulus, to me at any rate. However I was treated with great kindness by the majority of my colleagues. One of the latter Michael Hawkes, a few years younger than I who had the special distinction of appearing in the Oxford boat which ignominiously sank in the annual Boat Race against the premier University in 1951, ultimately became Chairman of the Bank. It was Michael who was at the helm when the decision was made to go for the new financial world created by 'Big Bang', the removal of barriers between the various activities of the Stock Market. It was a mighty move entailing the buying of a stock broker and 'jobber', the establishment of a massive dealing room (altered at huge expense several times) and engagement of hundreds of some-what yuppy personnel. It cost KB a vast fortune, the justification for which in the words of the Chairman was 'Either we go for it or we consign ourselves to the Second Eleven.' The corporate financiers in particular were certain that the entry into the securities market was essential to protect their underwriting business. It was a singularly interesting episode to watch and, not least, to experience the hitherto lightly occupied underground garage of 20 Fenchurch Street filled

With the Duchess of Gloucester at the naming of Dana Anglia, *Port of London 1978*

With Jim Lovell, the great hero of Apollo 13 (played by Tom Hanks in the film of that name). He had been twice round the moon – *a wonderful man*

With Terence (later Lord) O'Neill. Prime Minister of Northern Ireland

At the Dinner of the Institute of Chartered Shipbrokers. Among the group are Lord Sterling, Bill O'Neill (Secretary General, IMO), and myself on the far right

Opening the new passenger terminal in Amsterdam with Burgemeester Samkalden of Amsterdam and Eric Snowden, Captain of Chusan

with top-of-the-range Porsches, Mercedes and BMWs and to see the luncheon room filled with rather noisy young hustlers, coatless and wearing very broad braces.

My 'retirement' from Kleinwort Benson came in July 1988, strictly at the age of 60. The Bank had been very good to me although I never really fitted in with its style. The wonderful benefit that KB gave me was the opportunity to meet and work with a whole variety of business leaders – not just in transport – who gave me a hugely increased and broader knowledge of the commercial world.

I retired from KB in 1988 at a significant period in the Bank's story. David Peake, husband of 'Sukie' Kleinwort, daughter of Sir Cyril, was appointed Group Chairman. His tenure was fairly short. He gave way to James Cecil (later Lord Rockley) and subsequently

Simon Robertson, and these two between them skilfully arranged the sale of the once-proud premier Merchant Bank to Germany's Dresdner Bank. However that is tangential to my own story, other than that I had seen such a sea change as inevitable. Despite its significant past KB had neither the financial muscle nor the management to compete in the global market. It just might have retained its independence had it developed a niche of its own à la Schroders.

I had no intention of 'retiring' in the sense of assuming a life-style of golf and holidays. I was on the Board of some interesting companies, notably the British Transport Docks Board (which we saw through Privatization to Associated British Ports (ABP), possibly the most successful flotation of all) Transport Development Group (TDG) and TIP Europe the major Trailer Rental Company. Also I was, as a particular invitee of Leif Juul Jorgensen, another of my most treasured friends, an Advisory Board Member of J Lauritzen and DFDS Scandinavian Seaways of whose UK organization I later became Chairman. A very interesting task also was to be Chairman of the Anglian Board of British Rail at the invitation of Sir Robert Reid, my successor as President of the CIT.

CHAPTER 8

Life beyond work

IT IS BEYOND ME to continue this chronicle year on year and I think it better to devote some time to a general review of the main events and personalities of my life so far. In this account 'family' has so far taken somewhat of a back seat.

In our early days of marriage Hanny and I stayed on in my bachelor 'duplex' at 55 Campden Street. It was a very nice two bedroomed house with a communal garden and underground garage, thus ideal for a *small* family. Mariske had her early days there and quickly revealed her adventurous nature at the age of two by disappearing up stairways and crawling at high speed even up builders' ladders. She was, and still is, a wonderfully adaptable human being. However Campden Street could not be a long-term home and in 1976 we had to move to our current big modern-terraced house 'down the road' in Holland Park. It was stretching the finances, though prices of course were positively derisory compared with today. We sold Campden Street for I think £27,000. I guess today it would fetch upwards of £500,000, though a similar proportionate increase has benefited the Woodsford Square house. I suppose the lesson is, if at all economically feasible, never to sell on a house once acquired.

We had a steady 12-year stream of 'au pairs' to help us with the children. The score was two Danish, eleven Dutch (all friends, close and distant of Hanny's family) and one hopelessly spoilt Swede, who lasted two weeks before returning home to apparently much missed coffee mornings in Gothenburg. Our policy was to treat each of these wonderful young girls simply as an additional daughter, which meant that each of them would come with us on our holidays including on cruises to places as distant as the US, People's Republic of China, Russia, Japan or Indonesia and Malaysia. We were rewarded with marvellous help from the girls, many of whom remain friends with families of their own. Certainly saying good-bye to certain of them after their 12-month stint was a tear-jerking experience for all. Our own girls came along in 1974 (Mariske), 1978 (Katrina) and 1980

(Charlotte). They are an individual trio with different characters. They chose to go to different schools. Mariske wanted to 'board' and thus went to Queenswood where she excelled in Sport; Katrina did not want the boarding experience and entered instead St Paul's Girls School while Charlotte had a happy time at Francis Holland. There is quite a story attached to each. I encouraged Hanny to look at Queenswood, for a special reason. I knew it to be beautifully situated and marvellously endowed with sports facilities. When we were interviewed by Mrs Butler the Headmistress, she asked, 'Why, Mr Davis, did you select Queenswood as a possibility?' and I truthfully answered, 'Because I had some lovely girlfriends from Queenswood and the school has a unique reputation for producing marvellous wives.' This outburst nearly made Hanny cross Queenswood off our list. Mariske had a tremendously happy time at Queenswood, excelling in all sports. A special delight is the number of contemporaries there who remain close friends. St Paul's was another story. It had and indeed has the reputation of being number one of all and that was exactly what Katrina wanted! She narrowly achieved the very difficult entrance requirements, having excelled at Norland Place as head girl. On reflection I am not at all sure that she and we made the right choice for her. St Paul's is a school whose pupils (Paulinas) all come from the very top level of academic ability. This makes for a rather uneven society with great peer pressure and a scratchy environment. The school itself is pre-occupied with scholastic success, while other achievements (Katrina was Victrix Ludorum in athletics and also Captain of Lacrosse, Tennis etc) were not greatly valued. The pastoral care appeared to me to be slight and Katrina steadily lost much confidence. She was in the bottom quartile of academic achievement. Consequently she did rather less well than she might have done in a school of less 'hot-house' atmosphere. It came right again at the University of Wales in Cardiff, where she achieved a good 2:1. Katrina, who is blessed with somewhat unusually remarkable good looks was very shy as a little one. Partly to remedy this Hanny allowed her to become a child photographic model. She had exceptional success, gracing the cover of *Women's Weekly* on several occasions and also being the backdrop for both M&S and WH Smith in their children's departments. She could have carried on modelling but was dead against continuing in what she felt was a vacuous profession!

Charlotte went to Francis Holland where in her somewhat easy-going style she exhibited her great latent artistic ability and made troops of friends. She developed her extraordinary ability to get on with all manner of people, plus her determination and courage to try anything (from scuba diving to, horrors, bungy jumping; this characteristic she shares with big sister Mariske).

On top of these, the most important, family interests there were the various involvements, already referred to, and the Chairmanship of IMIF, which I had already taken on in 1981.

DFDS UK, through its excellent managing Director Ebbe Kohle Pedersen, offered me accommodation on the upper floor of the company's Passenger Office in Hanover Street at a most kindly rent, so I, with the IMIF Secretary Bengt Molin and my secretary Marilyn moved there straight away. It was very pleasant to be stationed in the West End, so much less aggressively frenetic than the City and so handy for the clubs and shops.

Before leaving KB I had been invited to join the Board of Tip Europe, the trailer leasing company, which had been the subject of a

The family in 1982

The family at nephew Nick's wedding in Santa Barbara: Katrina, Mariske, Charlotte and Hanny, 1993

With Katrina in Portugal

management buy-out. There was tough competition in the trailer leasing activity led by Tiphook, an unfortunately confusing similarity of name, which was headed by young and ambitious Chairman Robert Montague. Montague was one of those all too familiar entrepreneurial figures who seemed to value market share over bottom line profitability. This mentality led to rate cutting. The upshot was that Tip itself ran into a severe problem with its own loan agreement and broke its covenants with the biggest of its syndicated loans.

I had been on a trip, shipping related, to the Far East. I stepped off the plane at Heathrow after an 11-hour flight from Beijing to meet the Executive Board Members of Tip who rapidly explained to me the state of the company and said that I would have to take over the chairmanship immediately. A minor extra feature was that the Annual General Meeting was scheduled for two days later! Such a thing concentrates the mind wonderfully. In the event it was not so very difficult.

The unhappy creditors, the banks, had little option but to give me and my chosen new executives the chance to settle down and make the company sound. My only other non-executives at the time were two representatives of the Venture Capital Banks who had inspired the management buy-out and subsequent flotation. Thus, excellent as they were, they had their particular personal agenda of rapidly getting the company back on its feet and then exiting as fast as possible. I was very sorry indeed for the original three executives who had conducted the management buy-out. Sadly the market demanded that they should go, which was a bitter blow for all of them, particularly the very nice and honourable Chairman. My first thought was to find a new Finance Director who I hoped would quickly take over from me the role of Chief Executive. Here I somehow played a master-stroke of selection. David Callear had been Finance Director of one of Tip's subsidiaries. He was a young, blunt-speaking Yorkshire man and a quite brilliantly equipped accountant. Far from being a 'bean counter' David revealed a grip on organization, management and marketing and, above all, of the operation and sentiments of the City and Stock Exchange.

Together we returned Tip Europe to profitability and when this happened there came on the scene the monolithic entity of GE Capital who expressed a desire to buy the company.

This determination was resisted by David and me (a tactical move!) and we ended by extracting from GE Capital a higher price than they first offered. Thus I, and to a greater extent, David Callear, could take some credit for saving Tip Europe and its shareholders from a most problematic future. Indeed the shareholders achieved a conclusion that they could not have possibly hoped for a few years back.

The eighties and nineties were enjoyable years. Among my many preoccupations that of being Chairman of the Anglian Board of British Rail brought special problems. These Regional Boards instituted by Sir Robert Reid, who incidentally had succeeded me as President of the Chartered Institute, were designed to give useful 'local' knowledge of specific regions plus general advice to the general managers of the individual regions. We had no executive power, just strength of persuasion. I managed to recruit a wonderful team – Michael Falcon, the Chairman of Norwich Union, Lord Bridges, a former Ambassador and son of a distinguished Secretary of the Cabinet, Dame Paddy Ridsdale (who Ian Fleming took as his template for Miss Moneypenny in his James Bond stories), Mark Schreiber, a financial journalist who later became Lord Marlesford, an excellent NUR (now RMT) Trade Unionist, and Richard Onions, a cerebral merchant banker. We took our Board duties very seriously and incidentally took great joy in seeing 'our' main metropolis station Liverpool Street transmogrified from a filthy (the filthiest) railway terminus into the most interesting, cleanest and best. The credit was certainly not ours but we took delight in seeing what the real heroes had achieved with virtually no interruption of services and no serious casualties or deaths among the 250,000 passengers who passed through the station daily.

Improvements were achieved throughout the Anglia Region until the day came for the 'new' privatization and our term of appointment abruptly ended. As a final throw we asked the then Secretary of State for Transport John MacGregor for dinner at the private apartment of Norwich Union in London. It was especially appropriate since John MacGregor was MP for Norwich and obviously Michael Falcon was a mighty figure in the town.

We put forward our objections to the proposed break up of the railways into Railtrack for the permanent way and a whole posse of 'franchisees' who were to bid for the various passenger and freight routes. We expanded on the problems, not least of liability, that would arise under such a system and recommended a geographical break-up instead. We said that we had a Board in place and had identified the key executives for such a company. John MacGregor listened attentively and warmly commended our proposals but ended by saying 'Thanks, but no thanks'. The beautiful theoretical matrix which had been produced by the Civil Servants and their economist advisers had already been agreed by Government. And that was that. Alas the passage of time has proven that some of our worst fears were valid.

I was also Chairman of SITPRO (the Simplification of Trade Procedures Board) for 11 years. This excellent organization or quango was set up by an earlier Conservative Government and the first Chairman was Peter (later Lord) Thoneycroft. There was a first class team led by Ray Walker, totally committed to the elimination of paper and any other thing that hinders trade. It operated under a Grant-in-Aid from the DTI but due to its excellence and commitment was steadily selling its services and reducing by nearly 50 per cent its Government grant. When the then Secretary of State Lord (David) Young paid us a visit he expressed himself so satisfied with what he saw that he had no wish to come again. 'You are doing superbly: just keep it up!' were his departing words to me.

This success did not however seem to please our civil servant masters at the DTI who first of all decreed that we must sell off our Documentation Section (which was becoming very profitable) and at a later date instituted an in-depth report on the whole organization and its future. This report, carried out by a DTI civil servant, concluded that SITPRO had grown and assumed responsibilities and an international profile beyond its original conception. It was, I honestly feel, an expression of the Civil Servants' apprehensiveness regarding this tightly run, inexpensive quango. SITPRO exists still but with a very limited remit.

I had a splendid Board, carefully selected, during my 11 years as Chairman of SITPRO and was rewarded on retirement with a colour print of Turnberry Golf Course donated by the then Minister at the DTI, my old friend Stanley, Lord Clinton Davis. It seemed rather scant acknowledgement of so many years of hard endeavour! During that period I had also undertaken two terms as Chairman of the 'Europros' consisting of the continental equivalents of SITPRO. As SITPRO we provided the impetus to those continental organizations who consisted not only of EU members but the then constituents from the EEC. A particular friend of mine was the leader of the Czech organization, an aristocratic style of man whose family pre-war had considerable estates. The latter were of course taken by the Communists and throughout the Communist rule he was subjected almost nightly to aggressive questioning and humiliation lasting well into the early hours of the morning. He told me with some irony that his interrogators were still after Glasnost to be seen living an apparently prosperous life on the streets of Prague. No sanction or punishment had been implemented against them for their years of oppressive bullying, and worse.

I sensed the same resentment myself when, on two occasions, visiting the dread East Germany's Leipzig Fair. The DDR was one of the most unpleasant places I have ever visited combining, as it did, Communist oppression with German efficiency. It was interesting to watch the deference accorded by their Communist friends to two English MPs, Ian Mikardo and Joan Richardson. Mikardo conducted considerable trading business with the DDR which was no doubt highly profitable in a good capitalist way and he was very much at home among his drab Communist friends. It is hard to explain to those who have never lived under nor seen the nature of a country under total Communist rule just how colourless and concurrently frightening it was. No paint had been applied to the beautiful buildings since before the war. There was no joy in the demeanour of the unhappy citizens and the Stasi (Secret Police) were everywhere to ensure that no inappropriate comments ever were made. The important people in the regime were the Communist Party members who, with their ugly little lapel badges prominently worn, carried more weight and power than their theoretical bosses.

The years leading the C I Transport and SITPRO taught me a great deal about dealing with our own politicians and even more about the nature, habits and mind set of *some* civil servants. The Department of Transport was generally (as were its successive Secretaries of State) efficient and helpful. The DTI, on the other hand, had in earlier years, as the Board of Trade, great and diverse responsibilities including running many, now privatized, authorities and companies. Today, by contrast, it has mainly a regulatory duty plus the task of spearheading the country's export effort, the latter something for which it is stupendously ill-equipped. Why oh why must we continue to maintain these monolithic ministries to do

Chairman of EUROPROS at their Luncheon, April 1994, with the Duke of Kent, Patron of the Institute of Export

things which would be much better undertaken by the private sector? I spent six years as President of the Institute of Export, which underlined this.

IMIF, my particular 'baby', has maintained its momentum over all the years. As I write it is approaching its thirtieth Anniversary and my term as Chairman its twenty-fifth, to which must be added some three years as Hon Sec. It has been a most rewarding experience, entailing considerable diplomacy keeping together the disparate group who make up the diaspora of the maritime industries. For many successive years I led a group of members on a Far East trip to China, Hong Kong, Japan, Korea, Taiwan and Singapore. Our principal objectives were to discuss the dangers of overbuilding, and the need for concerted action to deal with that problem plus the multitude of hazards arising from pollution, governmental and super governmental regulation and the increasing litigiousness of the maritime world in particular and the world in general.

Scrapping was another item to be encouraged on the premise in particular that China was blessed with three advantages:

1. An enormous limitless market for the re-rolled steel in order to progress its deficient infrastructure.

With Mr Ogawa in Beijing in 1989

With the delightful Gregorios, Archbishop of Thyateira and Great Britain,
at an IMIF dinner in 1999

2. Abundant labour.
3. A vast coastline for the establishment of demolition/recycling sites.

The China National Shipbreaking Corporation were very appreciative of our efforts. It is interesting to muse that the then Chairman Mr Ma said that if ships for scrap went above $125 per light weight ton then the process would become uneconomical. Today, 2004/5, the cost has topped *$400* per ton.

The Chinese also assisted in endeavours by me and Gerald Cooper, formerly Director of Shipping for the State of Liberia, to set up a scrapping unit in Monrovia, Liberia, a worthy objective to provide useful employment in that already beleaguered country which paradoxically was and remains the home of the world's second largest ship registry. The registry is however fundamentally a US organization which merely remits a net amount to the Liberian government.

Atlantic Shipbreaking, its high sounding name, was not much of a success. The Chinese, who visited Monrovia to provide expertise, were systematically robbed by locals including, amazingly, policemen and soldiers. When protests were made they were met by bland governmental statements that nothing could be done really because the offending policemen/soldiers were 'off duty at the time'! The total of ships dismantled there remained stubbornly at *one*.

The 'City'

I had, until the early 80s, not taken any special interest in 'the City'. However, I was in the late seventies persuaded to join The Worshipful Company of Shipwrights, first as a Freeman and then as a Liveryman. Having joined rather late, and there being in the Shipwrights a convention that the 'Prime Warden' must be under 70 years old when assuming office, I realized I could not aspire to that high-profile position so I have remained on the Court, slowly creeping up the ladder to being the Senior Member (barring Prince Charles who has automatic precedence!) of the Court who has *not* been through the Wardens/Prime Warden mutation. It is an enjoyable institution with a significant proportion of the maritime community involved and the dinners are good meeting places with occasional good speeches.

My other principal Livery, which I joined mainly through the intercession of my good friend the late Pat (Lord) Limerick, is The

*Master of the World Traders in the Lord Mayor's Show. 'Like your motor!' said a voice.
'It's my wife's shopping car,' I replied*

Company of World Traders, one of the new boys ranking 101 in the Livery League, sandwiched between the Information Technologists and Water Conservators. I was Master in 1996 when Roger Cork (also a member) was Lord Mayor. My 'objective' as Master was to increase membership and this was achieved and the Livery is now in very good heart with Nigel Pullman as its superb Clerk and with a steadily increasing charity 'pot'.

A final livery enthusiasm is The Honourable Company of Master Mariners, a most clubbable entity who were kind enough to enrol me as an Associate Member despite my not having a Master's ticket nor having been in command of a vessel. The Masters of this Livery have quite regularly come from the P&O Company and the Headquarters ship *Wellington* has a splendidly warm atmosphere. Sea-going folk have a special aura of camaraderie.

Then there is the Corporation of Trinity House of which I am proud to be a 'Younger Brother'. In my late 70s 'Young' is a title that I cherish. Trinity House had a wide variety of duties to provide navigational aids all round the English and Welsh coasts (including pilotage, now hived off to the individual Port Authorities). However the provision of lighthouses, lightships and buoys remains Trinity House's responsibility and the main 'station' for the organization and home port for its tenders *Patricia* and *Mermaid* is Harwich, my own ville natale. So much, including lighthouses, lightships and buoys has been automated in recent years that the number of employees, which, pre-war, was substantial, has been dramatically reduced. The elimination of individual lighthousemen has resulted in a large number of dramatically situated − if occasionally very remote − lighthousemen's cottages being rendered empty and available for other work. I was asked by the then Deputy Master, Sir Patrick Rowe (The Duke of Edinburgh has the title of Permanent Master) to chair a company called Trinitas Services Ltd which would be responsible for letting out these little cottages (which had to be maintained and/or sold). The idea was to turn a liability into a 'face washing', even profitable, economic venture. This has progressed well and with Rural Retreats as our contracted marketing organization occupancy has been steadily improving. In fact Trinitas Services had finally been established under my chairmanship to be a consultancy company in the marine field employing the combined brains of our long list of Younger Brethren.

Danish UK Chamber of Commerce

Having over a period of years been on the boards of a number of Danish companies (DFDS, J Lauritzen, Hempel, 2M Invest, Shipserve etc), I was asked in 1992 to become Chairman of the Danish UK Chamber of Commerce. This was a very nice appointment further strengthening my many years' long affection for everything Danish, starting from my holiday in Copenhagen in 1949 and stimulated by my friendship with the beautiful Ulla Regenburg (here to study English life and institutions) at Cambridge in 1951. Trade between the UK and Denmark is – as with most trades with continental Europe – rather badly out of balance. Butter, bacon, Carlsberg beer, Bing & Grohndal and Royal Danish porcelain, Akvavit, Bang & Olufsen etc etc are all products which have a great market in the UK, but there are few UK exports which have the same appeal. Nevertheless the cultural and spiritual links are profound.

I therefore felt that the greatest trade contribution the DUCC could make would be to bring together the two communities to debate and face up to the major issues of the day; especially important since the Danes with their 5 million odd population carry a weight of influence and affection way beyond their size. Their views can be listened to and their efforts at social re-engineering can be carried out without seeming to be a threat to anyone else.

Danes are essentially happy people, particularly those from the Western Island of Jutland. Their only deficient national characteristic is what a Danish author annotated as 'Janteloven'. Broadly translated this means 'Keep your head down' or 'Who do you think you are?' Danes have a deep concern about high profile characters who, it is perceived, consider themselves better than others. These must immediately be cut down to size however truly distinguished and successful they may be. For instance, and not just due to the absurd tax levied on cars, no one in Denmark drives an expensive car.

The receipt of a Danish honour is a delight. I was honoured by being created a Knight Commander of the Dannebrog, a wonderfully distinguished order created in 1226! The Ambassador in London did the investiture but it is incumbent on the recipient to choose an appropriate day to go to Rosenborg Palace in Copenhagen to thank the Queen in person for the Honour. This I did and each Knight

With the Crown Prince of Denmark in 1997

Commander is ushered into a separate room to meet the seated Queen in private. Before going in I asked the Lord Chamberlain if it would be appropriate, that is not lèse majesté, to show her Majesty a photograph I had with me of my father greeting the young Princesses and their mother Queen Ingrid disembarking from DFDS *Kronprinsesse Ingrid* in the 1950s. I could hardly have imagined her very charming reaction. 'How lovely!' she said. 'I was *so* excited on that day, my first visit to England. How I remember it! Can I keep it?' Not in any case being disposed to deny a Queen, I was of course delighted to leave it with her. It was what I had anticipated.

The meeting in its total informality was rather touching and seemed to go on for so long that I sheepishly suggested that perhaps I should leave now because there was a large crowd in the waiting room yet to be admitted. She just laughed and said 'You are so right but thank you again for the photograph.'

I was naturally gratified to receive a CBE in the 1988 Birthday Honours. The citation was I recall for 'Services to Shipping'.

The Honours System seems to me to have been downgraded under the Blair Government . . . but maybe I should not indulge here in my acerbic thoughts about that.

The Marine Society

The Marine Society, founded in 1756, had a proud history. Its tasks included education of sea-goers, training (two former inshore survey ships gave many young people – principally Sea Cadets – the opportunity for 'Sea Time'), looking after retired seafarers who had fallen on hard times, supplying libraries to ships, etc etc. However with the diminution of the UK fleet and consequently number of seafarers the Marine Society saw fit, some 10 years after my chairmanship, to merge with the Sea Cadet Association, and the latter has more or less taken the whole organization over and its proud name and history has eventually disappeared. Probably this type of integration was inevitable; but as with all such 'mergers' it carries a hint of sadness.

Some thoughts on cruising

One of the most important developments on the passenger side of P&O in the early sixties was the development of 'Orient and Pacific Lines' as the service was temporarily called; this to soothe the susceptibilities of the then separately run Orient Line. Already the mighty development in the airline industry, consecutively the introduction of the Bristol Britannia (the 'Whispering Giant') rapidly followed by the brilliant Boeing 707 and Douglas DC8, forecast the demise of the great passenger liner as a mode of transport. The answer could only be to develop new routes and to treat cruising as a primary activity rather than a diversion from the regular trade routes.

Thus 'Circle Pacific' voyages were planned and rapidly became very popular. It however needed a powerful man, a US citizen, to head the development and marketing of this very different operation. He was found in the person of Warren Titus, then the Shipping Manager of Theo H. Davies our agents in Hawaii. It was a brilliant choice, initiated by Keith Geddes, and enthusiastically endorsed by me in particular and the Board. Keith was the younger brother of Ford and was earlier the Scotland and Cambridge Rugby Captain and a famous Night Fighter Flight Commander in the Squadron of 'Cats' eyes' Cunningham.

Warren Titus was, indeed still is at 91, an amazing man. Super-charismatic, he was a team-leader of epic style. He immediately became one of my greatest friends and I did my utmost to help him through the resistance posed by the old school of P&O and Orient Directors who were terrified of the inevitable part-Americanization of the on-board management of the ships. Such items as the supply of 'face cloths' (flannels), iced water at the commencement of every meal etc etc were looked on at first as so much vulgar flim-flam and unnecessary expense!

Some (only) of our Captains, who generally were gentlemen of great presence and importance, were not especially attuned to the leisure nature of Cruising. These latter exceptions were in fact pretty tyrannical. One such was of the opinion that late night revelry was inappropriate in 'his' ship. To ensure this, the mini combo of a band stopped playing, the bars were closed and occasionally as a final measure the public room lights were turned down at 11 p.m.! He had to be enlightened after one such trans-Pacific voyage where particularly the American passengers were totally confused by this regime!

Incidentally after leaving P&O Warren Titus effortlessly became the doyen of US cruising. Via American President Lines he formed and headed Royal Viking Line and later Seabourn Cruises, both superb niche operators. Finally he became consultant to Micky Arison, son of Ted, the entrepreneurial head of Carnival Corporation.

I personally find it amusing to list the ships on which I have travelled on both 'Line' voyages of old and cruises:

Corfu	*Canberra*	*Anking*
Himalaya	*Orsova*	*Galileo Galilei*
Chusan	*Iberia*	*France*
Oronsay	*Cathay*	*Oriana* (Mark 2)
Orontes	*Chitral*	*Britannis*
Oriana (Mark 1)	*Sangola*	*Amerikanis*
Achille Lauro	*Seabourn Pride*	*Clelia 2*

Scandinavia *entering New York for her christening, at which I was MC with the delightful task of looking after the ship's 'godmother', Liv Ullman!*

Meridien	Vistafjord	Crown Dynasty
Zenith	Braemar	Song of America
Century	Black Watch	QM2
Summit	Enchantment of the Seas	Spirit of London
The Victoria	Splendour of the Seas	Pearl of Scandinavia
Victoria	Brilliance of the Seas	QE2
Horizon	Song of Norway	Boudicca
Royal Viking Sea	Nordic Prince	Scandinavia
Norway	Jewel of the Seas	Patricia (T.H.V.)

Since the early seventies cruising has simply taken off. No longer is it the province of the well-heeled middle class, but is the choice holiday of all. An increase from 40,000 'cruisers' from the UK in the late sixties to 1,000,000 + in the new century is truly phenomenal.

I feel that the reason is very simple. As each holiday destination becomes more crowded, a ship with all its facilities has become a destination in itself and has the supreme attraction of being a moving hotel. As the brochures proclaim 'Nothing quite compares with cruising. Once on board, unpack your suitcase, relax – and let the world come to you.' Having only recently returned from 14 days on a 3-star ship where we were seated on a table for *eight* I can vouch for the eclectic mix of today's 'cruisers'.

I have maintained my involvement with cruising through Pearl Cruises of Scandinavia, a joint venture between Lauritzen and Skaugen which pioneered cruising in China, Indonesia and Japan, of which I was Deputy Chairman. And the current proposed Indian Ocean Cruises based in Goa and with a small ship, sailing on a special route to the Maldives and Laccadive Islands; it is a venture by the Foresight Group (Ravi Mehrotra) and one of which once again I am Deputy Chairman.

Afterthoughts P&O

I mentioned earlier that I would return briefly to the subsequent history of P&O after Jeffrey Sterling became Chairman.

At first it was as though sunshine had been released into murky corridors. Sterling Guaranty Trust (Sterling's lesser empire) was 'reversed' into P&O and an energetic team to run the old company was put in place. In particular P&O Cruises/P&O Princess Cruises acquired new and exciting vessels. All other activities were either stimulated or, if thought to be chronically unprofitable, sold off or abandoned.

Sterling himself surrounded by P&O historic paraphernalia became understandably seduced by his new position as Head of one of the UK's most historic and fascinating companies (one of the very few with a Royal Charter which enabled it to trade under the simple name P&OSN Co. . . . no Ltd necessary!). One Peter Thomas whom in the early sixties I had taken on as Press Officer, in which position he had been a very good and a loyal friend to me, became an effective PR promoter of the new P&O image. Thomas was ultimately rewarded by Sterling with a seat on the P&OSN Co. Board.

It is simply sad that by selling the cruising activity to the Carnival Corporation the venerable P&O SN Co, once indisputably the greatest brand name in shipping, became reduced to a middle-sized global port company with the residue companies of ferries, containers (P&O now only 25 per cent of Royal P&O Nedlloyd and later sold to AP Moller/Maersk)plus road transport, all likely to be disposed of. Shareholder value has been greatly increased but at the cost of virtually destroying P&O.

Jeffrey Sterling eventually retired, trailing clouds of glory – he enjoyed splendid valedictory parties – and much of this was well earned. On the other hand what did he leave behind? P&O is a mere shell of its former self – the stockholders, including the Chairman and Executive Board, have made excellent capital gain – but at the expense of the virtual extinction of a wonderful company. Under its new Chairman, my old friend Sir John Parker, I once hoped it might revive . . . but no, it was too late.

Since writing this, P&O has indeed surrendered to a 520p share cash offer from Dubai. There was a brief confusion when Singapore appeared to be mounting a possible rival bid, but it is now all over. P&O, except as a brand name under very different owners (Carnival for the cruise ships and Dubai ports for the group activities, especially ports) has in reality sunk below the waves. I note that Jeffrey Sterling from retirement appears to think that the demise was inevitable and tends to blame it on short termism by investment fund managers and hedge funds. While still Chairman he sold the passenger activities and fleet as well as bulk shipping just before the latter enjoyed the biggest boom in maritime history. Let us remember that Carnival and even the mighty Maersk were comparatively small companies a little while ago. Why have they prospered and grown while P&O has melted away? The answer may indeed lie in the fact that the company was indeed apprehensive of the City and its analysts. Maybe shipping is not very well suited to be a quoted Stock (the buccaneering Greeks have no such constraints on their freedom and speed of action), but it is interesting to muse what would have happened if the Board had fought harder for the long term future of P&O rather than feel obliged to sell off the company in bits. Clearly they unduly feared the wrath of the institutions. I just wonder!

It could have been so very different.

With Captain Panagiotis Tsakos and Admiral Lee of Taiwan at the Bureau Veritas meeting in Paris 1993

An amazing fluke. At a Bureau Veritas meeting in 1998 at the Wine Museum in Paris I got all the questions right and was created a 'Master of Wine'!

The Greeks

Back in the sixties Donald Anderson took to writing an irregular 'Chairman's letter' which he sent to seniors round the world and to the ships. After a maritime conference held in Athens I remember him writing 'The mantle of the great ship-owning merchant venturers has undoubtedly fallen upon the Greeks.'

I quickly endorsed those sentiments when I moved on to be Shipping Finance Director of Kleinwort Benson. The enthusiasm, opportunism, industry and sheer speed of decision-making was deeply impressive to me as was their dexterity in dealing with bankers and obtaining the finance they needed for their ships' purchases (sometimes as much as 110 per cent!). I was from my earliest days in Kleinworts much involved with them and my admiration has never diminished.

For instance Loucas Hajiioannou not only amassed Midas-sized wealth but also sired two very different sons, Polys who more or less maintained his original fleet, and the remarkable Stelios ('Serial Entrepreneur' as he describes himself on his visiting card) who conceived and originated his 'Easy Group' whose myriad companies' performance have admittedly varied from spectacular (EasyJet) to indifferent (EasyCinema). But Stelios's personal dynamism and inventiveness is astounding.

I have also had the privilege of working since my 'retirement' from KB with Captain Panagiotis Tsakos and his family, principally son Nikos. At an early stage they saw the benefit, indeed desirability, of creating public companies. The concept has grown to the extent that the quoted company TEN (Tsakos Energy Navigation), which figures on both the New York and Oslo Exchanges, has now achieved a market capitalization beyond $850 million. A vigorous high dividend maintenance plus a superb market has made it a darling of investors. I played a modest role in taking the Chair of the first quoted Tsakos Company. Alas the timing of this one – in dry bulk – was as unfortunate as the brilliant incorporation of TEN and its tankers was fortunate. However Global gave the entrepreneurial Tsakos Clan first experience in the governance of a public company and they were very fast learners indeed.

I assuredly admire the Tsakos family and cherish their friendship.

Mariske's wedding day. The whole family at the house before we left for church

The Far East

Never will I reduce my affection for the Far East, which affected me so greatly during my years out there. 'Too Far East Too Long' was a jokey description applied to Far Eastophiles. A recent late development was a telephone call from the Chairman of Hanjin, Sooho Cho, early in 2003 telling me that he was unhappy about the performance of Hanjin's Bulk Fleet and its representation and support from the Broking Committees in Korea and worldwide. Could I suggest and help with the formation of a dedicated Broker here in London? It was a fairly tall order but achieved within six months with the dynamic help of my good friends Michael Jolliffe and Norman Balbes and their majority owned broker house of Wigham Richardson. So Hanjin Eurobulk with state of the art offices in Sloane Street arrived of which I at the age of 76 undertook to be Non-Executive Deputy Chairman with Sooho Cho himself as Non-Executive Chairman.

Conclusion

How to conclude such a rambling set of thoughts as this little book contains?

Obviously it is to return to family. Hanny has been a marvellous wife and with great patience has supported and put up with her twenty year older husband, quite apart from producing three striking and wonderful daughters. The way Hanny adapted to life in the UK has been remarkable in itself because although so near in mileage terms, the style of the Dutch is very different from that of the British.

So there is the family, Hanny and our three wonderful daughters, the real product and linchpin of my 77 years to date. I hope I may be here for a few years yet.

I have been so lucky during my 56 years in shipping to have been witness to and participated in the greatest changes in shipping in centuries, for example:

1. The acceptance that shipping, though vitally important, is just a link in the chain of world commerce. 'Ship owning' is not an end in itself.
2. The emergence of up to 550,000 dwt, for example the Super-tanker/VLCC/ULCC replacing, say, the T2 'Standard' Tanker of World War II of 17,000 dwt.
3. 'Bulk carriers' of up to 350,000 dwt replacing the workhorse 10,000 dwt 'Tramps' for carriage of raw materials.
4. Ro/Ro (Roll-on Roll-off) vessels replacing in many trades, particularly Short Sea, the Lo/Lo (Lift-on Lift-off) vessels of yesteryear.
5. The introduction of containers and container ships. This perhaps most significant of all and completely taking over the 'Liner' trade.
6. The disappearance of Passenger Liners (point to point) but their replacement by staggeringly large and well-equipped Cruise Vessels. I remember my pre-war admiration for the *Queens* (81,000 GRT), *Bremen* (51,000 GRT), *Rex* (49,000 GRT), and *Normandie* (80,000 GRT), which are dwarfed now by such as *QM2* (157,000 GRT), *Freedom of the Seas* (160,000 GRT), and the projected Genesis Class of ships for RCCL which will be over *200,000* GRT.

Awarded 'Seatrade Personality of the Year', presented by the always delightful Princess Royal

Final Thoughts

As something of a show-off (my submerged acting abilities maybe?) many have I am sure thought of me and my career as something of a superficial piece of theatre; I guess justified to a large extent. But I would like also to be judged as someone who really did love and value his family, his friends all over the world – great and humble – his profession and the companies he served and, last but certainly not least, 'his ships'.

Reflections

I am a part of all that I have met;
Yet all experience is an arch wherethro'
Gleams that untravell'd world, whose margin fades
For ever and for ever when I move.

Ulysses, Tennyson

On reading through what I have written I feel I have done less than justice particularly to my home and private life. As a slight correction I have set out below a still incomplete list of those people who have been an influence in my life in its differing stages and places.

Early days (through 30s)

Parents and brother Roy . . . obviously
Miss Dunningham, St Francis Kindergarten, Cliff Road Dovercourt
John Chinneck, Ovingdean Hall Preparatory School
John Hills, Headmaster, Bradfield
John Moulsdale, 'G' Housemaster, Bradfield
Cecil Bellamy, 'C' Housemaster, Bradfield and brilliant play producer/director
Richard Hoare, friend at Bradfield. Later I was to be his Best Man
Bryan Whalley, friend at Bradfield and remains so to this day

40s

Bradfield and the RN (Bob Heycock with whom I joined up)
Adolf Hitler (his influence on life was beyond estimation!)
My friends the Boatmen and Fishermen of Harwich
Clare College – Sir Henry Thirkill, Master
Nick Hammond, Senior Tutor
Jim English
Dick DuCann
Geoff Weston
Peter Scowsill
Mike Edes

Cyril Horsford
George Law
Peter May (Pembroke)
'JJ' Warr (Emmanuel)

P&O

Well covered elsewhere but I must add my super colleagues in Japan, Nigel Burrage, Mike Connor (and definitely Zoriça his beautiful Serbian wife) and the Murrays, Tony and Valerie alone of these who are alive and remain among my best friends.

Hong Kong

Wong Chi Po our Chinese Compradore and all his family.
The Tung and Chao families and, particularly, Helmut Sohmen and the family of Y.K. Pao.
Robert Kuok of Singapore/Malaysia and Hong Kong. One of the most brilliant businessmen I have had the pleasure to meet and a charming companion.

London

In addition to those mentioned in the text colleagues like Kenneth Anderson, Peter Wise (a superb Personal Assistant and friend), Michael Penney, Sandy Stirling and innumerable Captains and sea staff (Wild, Hill, Wacher, Bradford, Gibb, Dunkley, Bodley, Riddlesdell Vickers, Lefevre, Edgecombe, Wood-Roe, Smylie, to name just a few of the Captains). Also Wolfram and Dorothee Nestel.

Kleinwort Benson

Above all Robin Fox who introduced me to KB but also the cerebral Martin Jacomb (one of great analytical mind and supreme 'bedside manner' when facing a problem!), Pat Limerick, John Macarthur and my original Shipping Department team: Geoff Orriss, Chee Jap, John Karriosifoglou, Stephen Pearson-Burton, and Stephen Brown. Also four of the finest secretaries any man could have in Pat Lofting, Tania Monham, Sally Grey and Jane Haile. Alas the last two have disappeared from my life and are devoted mothers of large families.

IMIF

My three Secretaries of IMIF each of whom contributed mightily and devotedly being overworked and underpaid in a very real sense: Hugh Relton, Bengt Molin, both sadly passed on, and Ian Bouskill who does not enjoy the best of health but remains to this day steady, meticulous and utterly dependable.

Home

Obviously my parents, long departed, and brother Roy, who died all too young, and his family who are almost as close as my own.

Don Harris – a craftsman of exceptional talent. He was very kind to my mother during her lonely days as a widow and for very many years worked on 'Summer Lawn'. Later he became the steadfast family friend of Hanny, me and the three girls. He positively renovated 'Summer Lawn' and was at his happiest working there and in the garden. Dying in 1989 he is still missed as our handyman, ornithologist and above all friend.

Maurice Scofield – he gained a 1st at Selwyn Cambridge. Poorish health prevented him from having a glittering commercial career; he always really wanted to write musicals and play the piano and organ in which he has astonishing talent. He is hard to explain but is a constant factor in the life of all the family. He is fun, fickle, a brilliant raconteur and encyclopaedia of funny stories. He is our great friend and Yorick who spends lots of time with us.

Leif Juul Jorgensen and family – my greatest Danish friend.

Our 13 (no fewer) 'au pairs' from Denmark, Holland and Sweden. They made everything so much easier bringing up three little girls. We treated each individually as part of the family and each came with us on holidays as far apart as China, the Caribbean and the Mediterranean. We had but one 'failure' – ironically the last and 13th who lasted only two weeks and could not settle down.

My mother-in-law Nel, Hanny's mother, who tragically lost Evert her husband in an accident when we had been married just three years, since when she has been a very regular feature in our lives, coming on at least one holiday every year with us. Surely a singular mother-in-law story!

Appendix 1

IMIF

The major Institution with which I shall always I think be associated, and indeed will always be happy to be, is the International Maritime Industries Forum (IMIF).

This came into being when the wise members, particularly among the shipowners, became aware that a crisis of unforeseen and previously inexperienced profundity had come about in 1974/5, the years immediately following the 'Yom Kippur' war.

The maritime industries found themselves in a state of deep crisis because of an over-supply of unprecedented proportions in ships, shipbuilding capacity, financial backing (a somewhat curious one that, one might think) and general pessimism.

Some very wise men, notably Jorgen Jahre, a delightful Norwegian tanker owner, who was Chairman of Intertanko, Robert Horton of BP Shipping, Otto Norland of Hambros Bank and Louis Vernede of AG Weser Shipbuilders, Helmut Sohmen of Marine Navigation and, tangentially Maersk McKinney Moller, came to the wise (if with hindsight, blindingly obvious conclusion) that this now chronic crisis could not be solved by the actions of one sector alone. Everyone involved must come together and work towards a solution.

Appendix 2

'To See Ourselves as Others See Us'

Some press cuttings over the years and some letters.

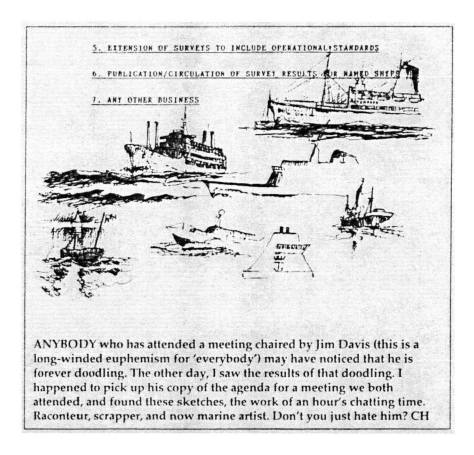

ANYBODY who has attended a meeting chaired by Jim Davis (this is a long-winded euphemism for 'everybody') may have noticed that he is forever doodling. The other day, I saw the results of that doodling. I happened to pick up his copy of the agenda for a meeting we both attended, and found these sketches, the work of an hour's chatting time. Raconteur, scrapper, and now marine artist. Don't you just hate him? CH

London Conference debates Europe

On 24 October 1995, the Danish UK Chamber of Commerce hosted a conference on the theme "EU/EMU – Boon or Disaster". The Conference was sponsored by Den Danske Bank and took place at the Hyatt Carlton Tower Hotel, Knightsbridge, London.

The highlight of the Conference was a debate by two of Europe's most outspoken politicians. Uffe Ellemann-Jensen, Denmark's former Minister for Foreign Affairs and a Member of the Danish Parliament, is fiercely pro-European, while Bill Cash MP for Stafford and Chairman and Founder of the European Foundation, is equally fierce in his Euro-scepticism. Chairing the debate was Jim Davis, CBE, Chairman of the Danish-UK Chamber of Commerce.

Uffe Ellemann-Jensen and Bill Cash are veterans of European politics, and both combine an ever-ready wit with a highly-developed sense of humour. And with Jim Davis in the Chair, the audience was assured of a debate to remember.

They were not disappointed and the debate was indeed lively in its discussion of the future of Europe seen from

From left to right: Uffe Ellemann-Jensen, Jim Davis and Bill Cash MP

the greatly differing viewpoints held by the two veterans of European politics. This topic is especially pertinent in the context of the Intergovernmental Conference on the future of Europe to be held in 1996.

It was an enjoyable and entertaining day with many delegates expressing their delight at the frank and enlightening exchange of views.

'LIKE THE WHITE RABBIT': Jim Davis' office reflects his frenetic professional pace, with pictures strewn on the walls, leather arm chairs and piles of paper everywhere, including the floor.

PHOTO: Nina Rangøy

Busiest man in shipping

Jim Davis, who will head up one of London's biggest shipping socials next week — the annual dinner of the International Maritime Industries Forum — can safely lay claim to being the busiest man in shipping.

His curriculum vitae leaves a reader dizzy: chairman of DFDS, chairman of Bromley Shipping, director of Associated British Ports, director of Global Ocean Carriers, director of Sedgewick Marine and Cargo, and director of Hempel Paints.

But that's just for starters. He is also chairman of the International Maritime Industries Forum (IMIF), chairman of the Simpler Trade Procedures Board, chairman of the UK-Danish Chamber of Commerce, president of the Harwich Lifeboat Society, vice president of the Marine Society and vice president of the Institute of Export.

And that's still not all. He is also on the council of the Missions for Seamen, trustee of the National Maritime Museum, and on the international committee of Bureau Veritas.

All this is not to preclude extra-curricular activities... Davis is a director of the British International Freight Association, fellow of the Royal Society of Arts, and vice president of Harwich & Parkestone Football Club.

His curriculum vitae also reveals that James Gresham Davis is a CBE (Companion of the British Empire), and lines up a veritable alphabet-soup of acronyms — MA, FCIT, FICS, FRSA, FNI (Hon) and FIFF (Hon) — after his name.

And that is to ignore the long list of organizations he has led in the past, such as the Institute of Chartered Shipbrokers, Institute of Freight Forwarders, Chartered Institute of Transport... and so on.

What is not on the list is the vast array of conferences he regularly speaks at or the number of after-dinner speeches he is asked to make. One of his shipping colleagues describes Davis as "a bit like the white rabbit in Alice in Wonderland — always rushing,".

No question, Davis certainly is BUSY. But why?

"I find it difficult to say no," he says. "I guess I have that fault.

"I don't want to sound boastful, but I suppose there are not that many articulate people in the shipping industry," he admits one autumn morning, nursing a painful toothache, but typically and over-gallantly squeezing in a quick interview before rushing off to an important lunch. He concedes he is not quite sure what the lunch is about but the guest list he shows off is certainly impressive.

With a CV that covers every conceivable area of shipping and transport and confidence in the scale of his own talents, it would be easy to imagine 65-year-old Davis as a stuffy and arrogant man.

The reality is rather different. He is certainly a dyed-in-the-wool establishment figure: Bradfield public school, Cambridge University, Law — and admirer of Margaret Thatcher. But he is also charming, humorous — and doesn't take himself too seriously.

His conversation is peppered with self-deprecating remarks, although he can talk seemingly without end, sometimes losing a listener in a morass of obscure detail. The constant demands for his time, however, verify his position as one of the industry's few real communicators.

Despite his professional demands and responsibilities, his busy life incorporates more than just the shipping industry. He married late, at 45, and has a relatively young family, whose picture occupies a prominent position in his small office.

His tuse, at the top of a Georgian DFDS building near Oxford Street, is like the cabin of a mad master's ship. There are pictures of the sea on the walls, leather arms chairs and piles of paper strewn everywhere, including the floor.

Davis is also a keen golfer and tennis player and is madly proud of his daughter's achievements on the racket game courts. Given half a chance, he will also rush out with a sketch pad to draw ships or the occasional landscape.

So how does he find time for all these activities? And is he not spreading even his prodigious talents slightly thin?

"When you cease to become a line manager, you can become a pluralist. The art is to know where to put your energies at any particular time. You know the expression, 'If you want something done, give it to a busy man.'"

After all this, Davis insists he is in semi-retirement.

Brought up in Harwich on the North Sea by a father who was a big wheel in Sealink Ferries, the younger Davis joined P&O straight after Cambridge. He spent years in Asia for the company before returning to Britain and later joining merchant bankers Kleinwort Benson in 1972.

After 13 years as chairman of IMIF, he has little intention of slackening the pace, but he insists he is aware of his age. "I'm a fogey," he says. "I've even got a (old age pensioners) bus pass."

So, if he could have done it over, would he have done anything differently?

"No, I don't think so. Mind you, I was unbelievably idle at school — I might have changed that. Listen, I must be off now," he says, as he rushes out the door.

By Terry Macalister

Adventures in wonderland

RABBITS seemed to loom disconcertingly large at the discussions of the International Maritime Industries Forum in London this week.

At the pre-dinner conference German banker Jurgen Bentlage, from Deutsche Schiffsbank, painted an arresting picture of his own kind. They had the heart of a rabbit (faint), the legs of a racehorse (to run away from projects) and, worst of all, the memory of an elephant.

Davis: a 'White Rabbit'

The self-mocking Bentlage admitted that shipping was not an altogether popular industry with bankers. With that sort of profile it would not be surprising if German bankers were not altogether popular with shipping people as well.

But that was not the end of the rabbit jokes. At the main event (the dinner) the ever-voluble Paul Slater got the proceedings off to what for some must have been a puzzling start by presenting Jim Davis, the forum's chairman, with a white and fluffy toy version of the self-perpetuating animal.

It was, he said, the Tradewinds (there, it wasn't that hard to say) Award for the busiest man in shipping, reflecting an article which pointed out the Davis propensity to rush — just like the White Rabbit in Alice in Wonderland.

The perceptive could probably identify the Queen of Hearts and the Mad Hatter as well. But we had better stop.

Table talk

JIM has fixed it again. In London last week, the big and the beautiful of shipping gathered for the annual dinner of the International Maritime Industries Forum. Audience marks out of ten for the jokes this year ranged from a miserable three to a fulsome eight. It didn't matter. Jim Davis has that rare ability of opening himself up to ridicule, yet retaining the respect of his peers. When another member of the top table at the dinner also held himself up to ridicule last week, he just looked ridiculous.

The IMIF bash is the best dinner in town. But even Jim Davis must be fed up with eulogies about the IMIF dinners. They are great, but so they should be. What is the point of having a dinner if it isn't enjoyable, never mind that most dinners aren't. Jim might even be a little tired of hearing how good the IMIF is. The IMIF, of course, has done a lot for shipping, but at the same time it has done nothing. It has benefited from having a truly charismatic leader, but this in itself has imbued the organisation with an aura of achievement that it doesn't deserve and doesn't look for.

The IMIF is a talking shop. That's what it does best. It can recommend solutions to shipping's problems because it has no axe to grind on any particular commercial block. The solutions, though, will have to be carried through by others, too many of whom enjoy the dinner and who mouth the IMIF dogma but understandably have no intention of doing anything unless it is for their own good.

The IMIF is a totemic crusader for common sense in shipping. Not the least important part of its function is to give the industry something to aim for. The industry itself will have to achieve the aims the IMIF sets for it. That message sometimes gets lost in the euphoria surrounding the organisation. And the great worry is that, when Jim retires, there will be nobody who can do the job half as well. Shipping will then march to the beat of a different drum. It won't be an improvement.

Davis takes on Global role

SHIPPING'S closest imitation of an india rubber ball, Jim Davis, has once again come bouncing back for more. His insatiable drive has seen him step up to the chairmanship of Global Ocean Carriers, the listed dry cargo scion of the Tsakos family's shipowning interests.

A director with the firm since its launch in 1988, Mr Davis will take over from Nabil Bahu, who is stepping down both as chairman and from the board. "They would have liked to have had me as chairman from the start," comments our own gentleman Jim, "but with all my other commitments it simply hasn't been possible."

A director of ABP, Sedgwick, Hempel and Tsavliris (among others), Jim will certainly have his work cut out. "It's an interesting time for the company, since we're taking advantage of a market that's going to face major changes over the years. We've high hopes to transform it into a major company."

So what of Jim's perennial efforts to help catalyse the shipping industry to see commercial sense through the International Marine Industries' Forum? "One has to keep trying," he says.

"It is an extraordinary

Davis: keeping busy

industry that just keeps on investing while failing to gain any return on capital, and that sees supply and demand dictate that the industry will always be out of balance. It desperately needs to sort itself out." Honest words Jim, yet again.

From world-wide shipping to home and family in Essex

PERSONALITY PIECE
by Don Black

Mr. Jim Davis with his daughter Charlotte, 4, at their Dovercourt home.

FRONKS Road, Dovercourt, has something in common with the Great Wall of China.

Both are long and distinctive enough to be seen from great heights.

Fronks Road by passengers in airliners to and from Heathrow, the Great Wall seen by astronauts.

Flying home from China, Mr. Jim Davis can pick out watchtowers on the wall, and his house, "Summer Lawn," in the road.

He was born there 55 years ago and still enjoys being in Harwich, along with his wife Adriana and their three daughters, Marieke, 9, Katrina, 6, and Charlotte, 4.

The town may be unfashionable to some people but Mr. Davis, newly-appointed chairman of DFDS (UK) Ltd and a major figure in the transport industry world wide, thinks it best for him.

Competition

"After a frenetic life attending meetings in London and overseas, coming back here is just right," he says. "My family can relax with me and my help to keep me feeling young."

Mr. Davis is a member of Harwich and Dovercourt Golf Club and also likes to play tennis and swim, encountering ever stronger competition from his young daughters.

Their home has a tennis court, but no swimming pool; that facility, he believes, has become too much of a status symbol and he can manage quite happily without one.

He survived as a bachelor until the age of 45, when he married Dutch-born Adriana. It was all foretold by a Chinese shipping magnate, the late Mr. C. Y. Tung, who gave Mr. Davis a love beam in Hong Kong and told him: "You will marry within 18 months."

And so he did.

DFDS comes under criticism for allegedly ruthless reaction to any competition that could threaten the group's dominance of North Sea trade.

"One does not mind rivalry," he insists. "We don't stifle competition — we meet it and better it."

DFDS (UK) is a subsidiary company of the Danish based group and will shortly move its head office from the City of London to Parkeston Quay. Mr. Davis is the company's first British chairman; might the group itself get more of a British element?

"I take the view that the British presence should grow," he replies. "The British flag is never ruled out."

DFDS burnt its fingers by trying, in a costly exercise to persuade Americans to take their cars in a luxury ferry from New York to Miami.

"It is not for us to speculate on the merits of a bright idea that did not take off," he suggests. "We can now concentrate on the North Sea, where trade is buoyant."

His own parentage indicates a knowledge of the business from childhood. His father was Col. Robert Davis, shipping and port manager at Harwich and Parkeston Quay from 1925 until 1951 apart from wartime duty as the Government's assistant director of sea transport.

Mr. Davis is a director of Associated British Ports (formerly British Transport Docks Board) and, in that role, is happy that Lowestoft has entered the container scene with the new terminal.

He is a council member of the Missions to Seamen, one of the participants in Felixstowe's pioneering ecumenical centre for seafarers.

Varied interests come together in his current presidencies of the Institute of Freight Forwarders and the World Ship Society. Mr. Davis is no mere

"All sorts of plans are being studied — the dispensation of ships and so on," he says. "There is a lot we can do."

"Egon Ronay gave five stars to our Dana Anglia on the Harwich-Esbjerg route, but one can never be content with one's product.

"Crossing the North Sea should not be something that has to be got over. Our evening entertainment has been upgraded, but mornings are still rather boring.

A 'first'

"Mornings should be just as much fun as the night before. There could be dancing, competitions and activity around the pools that are available."

DFDS (UK) is a subsidiary company of the Danish based group and more investment will go into DFDS services between Parkeston Quay and Germany, augmented this summer by a seasonal passenger and freight link with Cuxhaven.

figurehead, he knows the complexities of the forwarders' registration scheme that started this month and he can draw a ship so well that it could be the work of a professional artist.

He is a director of merchant bankers Kleinwort Benson Ltd, deputy chairman of London shipbrokers Harley Mullion Ltd and a director of Transport Development Group plc which has many subsidiaries in the UK and abroad.

Mr. Davis admits to speaking very little Danish or Dutch — DFDS and his wife are, of course, totally at home in English — but is fluent in Japanese, a result of long service with P & O in the Far East.

Master

He read economics and law at Clare College, Cambridge, after national service in the Royal Navy, and entered the shipping world as a Master of Arts.

Since then, it seems, he has been able to master the complexities of just about every commercial activity.

Later this year, a chairman of the International Maritime Industries Forum, he will lead a team to that region for discussions on shipping problems that appear to get worse by the month.

"All the marine industries are in disarray — rates and overtonnaging for a start — and we must have some order in shipping," he warns. "Benevolent capitalism brings results, with the potential of giving everyone a better life, but state subsidies can do a lot of harm.

"Whether his skills in trade and ability to get on with people at every level will have the desired effect in the Far East in 1984 remains to be seen.

MITSUI BUSSAN KAISHA, LTD.

HEAD OFFICE
6, 2chome, Nihonbashi Muromachi,
Chuo-ku, Tokyo.
YAWATA BRANCH
3-2 Edamitsu, Shintakasu, Yawatashi,
Fukuoka, Prefecture, Japan.

IMPORTERS ◆ EXPORTERS

ORES, IRON, STEEL, NONFERROUS METALS & FUELS

CABLE ADDRESS
"MITSUIBUSSAN OSAKA"
CODES
ACME & BENTLEY'S SECOND

OSAKA BRANCH
41, 2chome, Koraibashi, Higashi-ku,
Osaka.

Osaka, 5 April 1956

Refer to Your
Our

Dear Jane G. Davis,

Many thanks for your letter from Shanghai. It was just in time when I was hurrying to send you the pictures you are waiting. I am not clever enough to bring out in the picture the unforgetable atmosphere in that farewell party on the ship. However even though not taken skilfully, I may be very pleased if you will keep them in your album for the memory of the last day in Japan.

I have sent the pictures also to your English friends who are found in the picture, through Mr Sakamoto in your office in Kobe.

After leaving the ship on that evening Chibi chan could not walk along the dark cloudy wharf without tear on her cheek which to my regret I could not show you in photo.

I hope you will always be happy and loved by every people every time and everywhere like you were in Kobe.

Yours Truly
C. Endo

Translation from "Essays on Shipping –
Memoir of my Life in Daiichi Chuo Kisen "
written by Mr. T. Ogawa August, 1991

Translation from P.65–66

One of my unforgettable good shipping friends in London is Mr. Jim Davis, Chairman of IMIF.

About 10 years ago when I was Executive Vice President of our company and Chairman of Scrap Promotion Special Committee in Japan Shipowners Association, he visited Japan on IMIF Delegation Tour to the Far East for the first time and I, as Chairman of Committee, J.S.A. received him and his colleague.
We discussed the way how to overcome long lasting shipping depression.

Since then IMIF Delegation headed by him visited Tokyo to meet with MOT, JSA, SAJ (Shipbuilders Association of Japan), NK (Nippon Kaiji Kyokai) etc. every year around November.

Some years later, on my European trip, I visited his office which was next to our London office and we exchanged frank opinions on the necessity of promotion of scrapping under worldwide scale. He strongly appealed me for the support to IMIF as JSA, and if not even as Daiichi in order to encourage his campaign. I understood what he emphasized and for worldwide spiritual mobilization of Scrapping I promised to support him.

He has a wonderful talent to organize and conduct on Economic Orchestra consisting of the top leaders of world maritime industries.
He plays his splendid political – economic music at the gatherings of OECD, UNCTAD, IMO, INTERTANKO, INTERCARGO, BIMCO etc.

Someone in London once whispered me that he is a grandstand player, but I do not think so. He did many fine jobs for the common interest of various industries connected with world shipping and shipbuilding. Anyhow he is an able business talent.

He worked from his young age for P & O and was stationed at Hong Kong and Kobe as its representative during 1950s. He was a member of Hirono Golf Club and he knows well and loves Japan.
He sings "Ginza no Kankan Musume" much better than young Japanese.
I have been introduced by him many influential business executives in Europe who are supporting his activities strongly.

Through my experiences of joining IMIF Far Eastern Delegation to Tokyo, Peking, Hong Kong, Taipei and Kaohsiung several years ago, I could see well Jim's charming leadership with thoughtful considerations for the members of delegation who were English, Swede, French, German, Hong Kong Chinese and Japanese.

Many Japanese business top executives can receive Western business friends at their head offices of the company with the assistances of staffs and company background. However if they go out to Europe or The Sates to attend big international symposium or conferences alone, their company's names and title on their business cards will not help them so much as in Japan.

After all their social status, attractive personal characters and English speaking abilities etc. are more important.

Generally speaking many Japanese business executives are usually quite shy and hesitant to see and talk with foreign guests due to mainly their mental complex of poor English conversation ability, and they are likely to try to avoid such opportunities to meet foreign guests with some incomprehensible excuses.

Outspeaker Jim once told me, "Takeshi, tell me, with whom should we, European Shipping executives, discuss about Japanese shipping ?
After passing away of Mr. Ariyoshi, NYK, no reliable speaker or responsible negotiator for Japanese shipping exists from European shipping executives' point of view."

I believe, Mr. Suzuki, Executive Vice President, M-O Lines was appointed the Chairman of Intertanko for the first time in its and also Japanese shippings histories. We cannot deny regretfully that we have very few really international-minded Japanese shipping men with rare exception like him.

I think we should help him in Intertanko and learn from him more.

(End)

Appendix 3

The 'Doodle Habit'

A small selection of drawings, most of them done during board meetings.

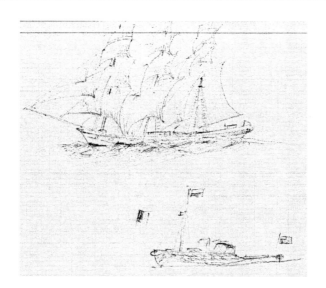

Ships alongside in Barbados.

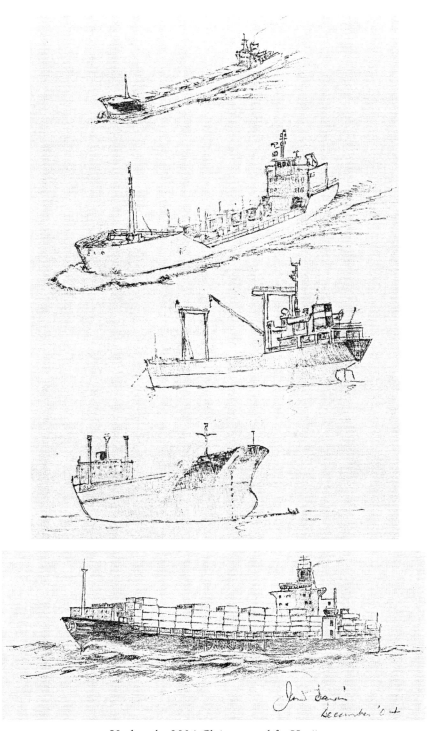

Used as the 2004 Christmas card for Hanjin

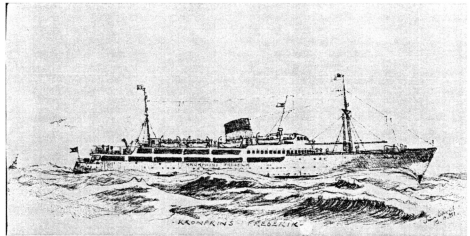

Done in 1951

Done in 1944 (aged 16)

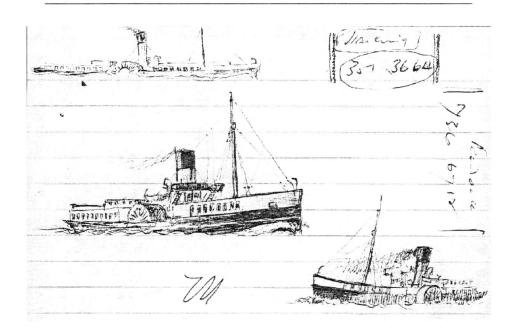

Index

148